D1276493

SELECTED POEMS OF
JONATHAN SWIFT

THE POETRY BOOKSHELF

General Editor: James Reeves

Selected Poems of John Donne
Selected Poems of John Clare
Selected Poems of Robert Browning
Selected Poems of Gerard Manley Hopkins
Selected Poems of Emily Dickinson
Selected Poems of S. T. Coleridge
Selected Poems of William Blake
edited by F. W. Bateson

English and Scottish Ballads
edited by Robert Graves

Selected Poems of John Dryden
Selected Poems of William Wordsworth
edited by Roger Sharrock

The Late Augustans
edited by Donald Davie

Selected Poems of Robert Burns
edited by G. S. Fraser

Selected Poems of Byron
edited by Robin Skelton

Selected Poems of P. B. Shelley
edited by John Holloway

Selected Poems of Tennyson
edited by Edmund Blunden

Seven Victorian Poets
edited by David Wright

Jonson and the Cavaliers
Eight Metaphysical Poets
edited by Jack Dalglish

Shakespeare's Sonnets
edited by Martin Seymour-Smith

JONATHAN SWIFT

SELECTED POEMS OF
JONATHAN SWIFT

Edited with an Introduction and Commentary

by

JAMES REEVES

BARNES & NOBLE, INC.

PUBLISHERS : BOOKSELLERS : SINCE 1873

First published in the United States by Barnes & Noble,
New York 10003
Printed in Great Britain by Morrison and Gibb Ltd
London and Edinburgh

CONTENTS

COMMENTARY AND NOTES

INDEX OF TITLES AND FIRST LINES

INTRODUCTION

I

SWIFT is one of those large, elemental figures in literature whose standing and influence cannot be defined or measured. Dr. Johnson was another. They bestride their times, appearing to be at once *of* them, yet apart from them. Literary history does not know whether to classify Swift as satirist or poet, controversialist or moralist. He is the sum of all these, and more. One, and only one, of his books is known, at least in part, to every child in the English-speaking world and beyond. But that he is most widely known as a writer for children is an accident and an irony that would have amused him. His poems are comparatively little known. That is the reason for the appearance of this selection. It is small, but representative, sufficient at least to show the variety and scope of his writing in verse, which runs through all the phases of his life and reflects every aspect of his diverse and complex personality. This is what, despite its 'occasional' character, gives it unity and interest beyond the merely occasional.

Jonathan Swift was born in Dublin on 30 November, 1667. He was descended from an old English family of Royalist sympathies, and was related by marriage to Dryden, the foremost man of letters of the older generation. His grandfather, the Rev. Thomas Swift, had been ruined during the Civil War by his loyalty to the King. His father, steward of a law society in Dublin, had married a Leicestershire woman, Abigail Erick. Some months before Jonathan's birth his father died; as a baby his nurse abducted him and took him to England, and he was not returned to his mother until three years later. To relieve her of domestic and financial care, Jonathan's uncle Godwin charitably maintained him, and at six years old sent him to school at Kilkenny. His mother returned to Leicestershire with her other child.

Brought up virtually as an orphan, Swift long resented the poverty, the lack of a real home, and the air of charity associated with his childhood. It made him bitter and introspective. As a refuge from unhappiness he read much. His favourite book was the Bible, which he studied without guidance; it may have been this which later made him one of the most original and unorthodox of great churchmen.

His early reading did not, however, make him a successful scholar. In 1682 he began his undistinguished academic career at Trinity College, Dublin, where he found the traditional curriculum irksome. He was granted a degree only through the indulgence of his superiors.

On the accession of William of Orange, Swift, now a young man of twenty-one, without means or prospects, left Ireland to seek employment nearer the centre of government. His mother secured him the post of secretary to Sir William Temple, with whom he had family connections. Sir William, a retired diplomat, lived at Moor Park in Surrey, and it was here that Swift passed much of his next ten years. He wrote, studied and performed the duties of something between valet and clerk to his employer; he met the leading political figures of the day, sometimes walking and talking with the King himself. Among the members of the household were Rebecca Dingley, a poor relation, and Esther Johnson, a young girl adopted by Sir William. Thirteen years Swift's junior, Esther—or Stella, as he came to call her—became first his pupil and then his companion and chief confidante in Temple's household. Their attachment, which was deep and intimate, lasted until her death. We know nothing of her except what Swift tells us, and he never revealed the truth about their supposed marriage. It seems probable that he married her secretly, but the two never lived together openly as man and wife. When she died in 1728, Swift was inconsolable, and never again mentioned her name.

At Moor Park Swift fretted for independence and distinction. His subordinate position irked him, although he respected and admired his master. In 1694 he took holy orders in the hope of making a living for himself in the Church and gaining preferment equal to his talent and ambition. For a short time he became a country clergyman at Kilroot in Ireland, but he was soon back at Moor Park, helping Sir William with his work and himself engaging in the first of the writings for which he was to become famous. He had already written poems on which Dryden was said to have commented: 'Cousin Swift, you will never be a poet.' *A Tale of a Tub* and *The Battle of the Books* were, however, brilliant prose essays in controversy. The former, which was theological in character, was important because it gained Swift a reputation for unorthodox religious views; and he always considered that it was one of the causes of his failure to gain a high place in the Church.

In 1699 occurred the death of Sir William Temple, his master, patron and friend. The various hopes which their association had led Swift to form were destroyed. At thirty-two he was a man with no settled direction in life, no definite prospect of promotion—or indeed of employment, yet a man filled with a restless and insatiable ambition, and endowed with great intellectual gifts. He must have appeared to his contemporaries as one not easy to get on with, for his pride and personal integrity made him touchy, even irascible. Yet to those friendships he formed—and they were with some of the greatest intellects and the finest spirits of his day—he was intensely loyal. The age of William and Mary, of Queen Anne and of George I was one of fierce political warfare, both Whigs and Tories struggling ruthlessly and often unscrupulously for power. Position and influence went to those who could best serve a party or a statesman. A man who might set his own principles above party, justice above expediency, and the interests of his Church above those of individual politicians might come to be regarded as dangerous.

For the present, however, Swift was almost unknown. Shortly

after Temple's death, disappointed in the promise of a position of some influence, he was obliged to accept the obscure living of Laracor, a village twenty miles from Dublin. His congregation was tiny, and his duties of the humblest. It is recorded that on one occasion his congregation consisted of his clerk alone, whereupon he began the service with these words: 'Dearly beloved Roger, the scripture moveth you and me . . .' The story may be apocryphal but it is characteristic. In Ireland he was forced to see the misery and poverty of the peasants at close quarters. Their condition aroused his fiercest indignation and kept burning in his heart the passion for justice and freedom which never cooled. He loved intelligence and liberty, and loathed stupidity and oppression. All his life he fought against them. His exile in Ireland, relieved as it was by the presence of Stella and Mrs. Dingley, whom he had persuaded to move from England, fretted his restless mind and did nothing to satisfy his ambition. Ambition, we are told, is the sin by which the angels fell; certainly it is a profoundly destructive passion. There is no doubt that Swift longed for power; he was not only a clear and able thinker, a forceful writer, a man of strong conscience and principles, he was also exceedingly practical and methodical. All his writings testify to this. His love of individual men and women —whatever he may have come to feel about mankind in general— made him one of the most consistently charitable and generous of Christians, so far as his poverty and his natural carefulness would allow. Obliged by circumstances to live a sedentary and inactive life, he had the temperament of a man of action. His biographers tell us that he was fond of violent exercise, and this must have been only partly due to the demands of health.

Of the ten years following 1700 Swift spent at least four in London. He frequented coffee-house society and became the friend of wits and writers. He got to know Addison and Steele, and earned himself a reputation as a witty pamphleteer and controversialist. He was taken up by the Whigs who needed the help of as many able pens as they could command. When they came to power in 1708, he had a right to hope that they would relieve him

4

of his Irish living and give him some position worthy of his talents and his services to the party. But he found that the price of preferment was betrayal of his Church. He was unswervingly loyal to the Church of England and strongly disapproved of Dissenters. The Whigs needed the support of the growing body of Dissenters and were prepared to make concessions to them. Swift could not find it in his conscience to endorse their religious policy. Accordingly, disappointed and still unpromoted, he drifted away from the Whigs and began to associate with the Tories. In particular, he formed close and intimate relations with the leaders, Harley (later Lord Oxford) and St. John (later Lord Bolingbroke).

In 1710 the fall of the Whig ministry and the triumph of the Tories brought Swift to the zenith of his power and influence. He was put in charge of the Tory paper, *The Examiner*, and his advice was sought continually by the most important men in the government. Oxford and Bolingbroke called him by his Christian name; he was the prey of suitors for every kind of favour. He used his influence unsparingly to help those whom he considered deserving. He betrayed no friend; and he employed his pen with skill and energy in the service of those principles in which he believed, and which he believed to be served by the Tories. He received no money for his writings, and no public recognition. Men who did far less than he for the party and the nation were rewarded with high honours; but still promotion failed to fall upon Swift. Bishoprics were in the gift of the crown, and Queen Anne and her advisers did not trust this brilliant but dangerous man.

In 1712 Swift suffered from a temporary breakdown in health. He was attacked by the fits of giddiness which later became more frequent and more painful, producing deafness, sickness, and the most terrible fits of morbid depression. From now on his health was never good for long. He lived continuously under the fear of insanity, a fear which in the end proved to have been prophetic. At the age of fifty, seeing an ancient elm with its topmost branches withered and leafless, he said to a friend: 'I shall be like that tree; I shall die at the top.'

An account of Swift's life in outline must to some extent represent him as a gloomy, morbid and dissatisfied man. But if he seems to have failed in all he consciously desired, he fulfilled himself in other ways. He enjoyed the friendship and esteem of the best minds of his time, both in London and in Dublin. His Irish friendships, more than those with English men of letters, were productive of much of his best verse. His writings were highly esteemed by connoisseurs. The years in London must have given him many hours of real happiness and pleasure. One of the less happy incidents which began during his years there was his friendship with Esther Vanhomrigh, recounted in the long poem, *Cadenus and Vanessa*, written for her alone and not printed during her lifetime. No doubt he was rash to encourage this passionate young woman in hopes which he could never satisfy. She desired ardently to become his wife, but he would not desert Stella. Yet he loved Vanessa, and her adoration meant much to him.

In 1713 Swift was rewarded with the Deanery of St. Patrick's, the Protestant Cathedral of Dublin. This preferment he regarded as banishment. After a short stay in Ireland he returned to London; but serious differences between Oxford and Bolingbroke made the fall of the Tories inevitable. In 1714 Queen Anne died, and was succeeded by George I. The Whig ministry was recalled. The Tories were out of office, and Swift's period of public influence in England came to an end. The remainder of his life is virtually the history of a disappointed man's exile in Ireland, relieved by occasional visits to England and solaced by the friendship of writers and wits and, for a time, the devotion of admiring women.

In 1723 the death of Vanessa after his final violent rejection of her caused him deep anguish and remorse. The following year he achieved considerable popularity among the Irish for his championship of their rights against the encroachments of English exploiters. At all times the condition of the Irish caused him savage indignation, yet he did not love Ireland. He saw too much misery, too much prejudice, and too much stupidity; and so far away from the centre of government he felt powerless to do anything to remedy matters.

6

It was during these years as Dean of St. Patrick's that he wrote the greatest of all his works, *Gulliver's Travels*, which was published in 1726 and earned him the immediate applause of literary and fashionable circles.

Yet it was never literary fame which Swift longed for, it was appointment to a position of power and influence from which he could do direct, practical and lasting good. On the accession of George II in 1727 he went to London in a final attempt to get an English benefice. When this failed, he left England, never to return. The following year, to his lasting sorrow, Stella died. He felt altogether alone in the world. His melancholy, his ill-health, his fear of madness increased. In 1729, in a letter to Bolingbroke, he wrote the terrible words:

> You think, as I ought to think, that it is time for me to have done with the world; and so I would, if I could get into a better before I was called into the best, and not die here in a rage, like a poisoned rat in a hole.

In 1731 he wrote one of the best known of his poems, the humorous, bitter *Verses on the Death of Dr. Swift*. Thoughts of his own death increased with age and failing health. For the next ten years he carried on his work as Dean with due regard to the interests of his office and the Church, and with unsurpassed charity towards those in need. His mind gradually gave way, his deafness and giddiness increased, he became more and more isolated from the world, sometimes hardly aware of what he was saying. In 1741 he was put under restraint, and in the following year guardians were appointed. Still he lingered on, and it was not till 1745, on 19 October, at the age of seventy-eight, that he died at the Deanery in Dublin.

He left about £12,000, with which was endowed a charitable institution in Dublin, St. Patrick's Hospital for Imbeciles. He was buried in St. Patrick's Church, in the grave where—to quote his own epitaph, carved on his monument—'savage indignation could no more tear his heart': UBI SAEVA INDIGNATIO ULTERIUS COR LACERARE NEQUIT.

II

If Dryden told Swift that he would never be a poet, there has been a tendency among later critics to echo him. Leslie Stephen, for instance, in late Victorian times said that his poetry might be called rhymed prose. Stephen was writing during the triumph of romantic ideals in poetry, and if we expect in the poems of Swift the qualities we associate with poetry from Wordsworth to Tennyson, we shall not find them. Swift was in certain important respects anti-romantic, but today we no longer regard this as a disqualification for a poet.

Dryden died in 1700, and up to that date he could be excused for his scepticism about the young man's future as a poet. Swift had written little in verse except the half-dozen Pindaric odes of the Moor Park period. This was the kind of poem which, under the influence of Cowley and his followers, a young man aspiring to poetic fame was expected to write. Swift had too original a mind to do this kind of thing well. Here is the beginning of his ode to his patron, Sir William Temple:

> VIRTUE, the greatest of all Monarchies,
> > Till its first Emperor rebellious Man
> > Depos'd from off his Seat
> > It fell, and broke with its own Weight
> Into small States and Principalities,
> > By many a petty Lord possess'd,
> But ne'er since seated in one single Breast.
> > 'Tis you who must this Land subdue,
> > The mighty Conquest's left for you,
> > The Conquest and Discovery too:

The poem is not altogether contemptible: beneath its contrived and conventional surface can be detected a moral earnestness which was perhaps out of key with the cynical temper of the times; but what made it unlikely that the writer of such stuff would ever become a poet in the fashionable sense was Swift's evident dissatisfaction with the artificiality, the note of false compliment which this style of verse imposed.

Yet Swift himself had no doubt that he had been born a poet: it was his times, not his temper, which were anti-poetic. In the verses he wrote at a much later date, *On Poetry: A Rapsody*, he speaks out with coruscating plainness about the incongruity of a poetic destiny during the period of the Revolution.

> Not Beggar's Brat, on Bulk begot;
> Nor Bastard of a Pedlar *Scot;*
> Nor Boy brought up to cleaning Shoes,
> The Spawn of *Bridewell*, or the Stews;
> Nor Infants dropt, the spurious Pledges
> Of *Gipsies* littering under Hedges,
> Are so disqualified by Fate
> To rise in *Church*, or *Law*, or *State*,
> As he, whom *Phebus* in his Ire
> Hath *blasted* with poetick Fire.

What destroyed Swift as a man and redeemed him as a poet was the impossibility of combining worldly success with the maintenance of poetic integrity as he conceived it. Born with a poet's instinct to tell the truth about society, but without the family influence necessary to give him security, he spent himself in the struggle for a position in the established church worthy of his gifts. But the establishment knew him for a man of integrity, a man dangerously liable to speak out against the abuses by which power was maintained, and Swift never had his reward in the field of worldly success. No doubt his ambition was incompatible with the poetic vocation, but he was cruelly, if unwittingly deceived by his Tory friends who fell at the death of Queen Anne. Her death was the death of Swift's worldly hopes. He was left to rail and rage in Ireland against the corruption, the self-seeking, the greed and cruelty of the political establishment which had not only cheated him of his hopes but acted against the interests of all the decent, humble people for whom, as a conscientious churchman and a man of sense and humanity, he cared. He strove passionately for the rule of reason and decency against self-seeking and corruption; but, being a poet, he was not himself altogether reasonable. It was illogical to expect the world to be anything but worldly. Yet there is no more convincing proof of his truly poetic nature than that he should have been prepared to destroy himself in the illogical effort to improve the world in which he lived.

His true poems are the fruits of his despair, not of his hope. He learned by the hardest way the futility of worldly ambition; he learned that its fulfilment would have involved him in the lies and flattery by which men of wit were obliged to maintain themselves in Augustan society. He preferred to preserve his truthfulness as a poet, his integrity as a Christian, and his dignity as a man.

The first quality to be noted in his poems, then, is their truthfulness. After the Pindaric poems he flatters no one, because flattery is lies. He has no use for the polite compliments which were the stock-in-trade of many versifiers of his time. His obsessive honesty, his almost morbid compulsion to truthfulness, is everywhere evident, as in the first trifle with which the present selection begins, *Verses wrote in a Lady's Ivory Table-Book*, composed when he was thirty-two. It is evident in the *Verses on the Death of Dr. Swift*, in which, at the age of sixty-four, he contemplates the effect of his own death on the friends he has loved and the society in which he has lived: there is no self-deception, no comfort in the usual consolations of illness. It is evident in his last terrible indictment of the Irish parliament, *The Legion Club*, written when he was nearly seventy. Even the risk of arrest did not deter him from telling the truth, as he saw it, about the corruption of Anglo-Irish politics.

Another aspect of Swift's passion for the truth is to be found in his interest in parody and burlesque. It was as necessary to him as breathing that he should show up conventional falsity of expression wherever he found it, whether in literature or in society. Many of his most effective prose satires—*Polite Conversation*, for instance, and *A Meditation upon a Broomstick*—are burlesques of this kind. Here he strips of their pretences the cant of social talk and the inflated style of fashionable moralistic writing. In verse the same impulse is behind the two excellent and celebrated parodies, *A Description of the Morning* and *A Description of a City Shower*, where Swift exposes the pretentiousness of manner in which humble and everyday subjects were clothed by artificial versifiers. Poems such as the amusing *Phillis, or the Progress of Love* and *The Progress of Beauty* are not primarily an attack on women; they are an attack on polite fictions about women, the anti-romantic deflation of false sentiment.

Swift has sometimes been attacked as a purely destructive writer, mainly negative in effect. This is to misunderstand both him and his times. There is a sense in which truthfulness, however unpleasant, however destructive in its immediate purpose, is always creative. Half a century after the death of Swift, Blake wrote:

> Thou hast a lap full of seed,
> And this is a fine country.
> Why dost thou not cast thy seed
> And live in it merrily?

> Shall I cast it on the sand
> And turn it into fruitful land?
> For on no other ground
> Can I sow my seed
> Without tearing up
> Some stinking weed.

Like Blake, Swift knew that if society is rotten with falsehood, that falsehood must be rooted out before it can receive the seed of truthfulness. He was undoubtedly possessed all his life of a vision of society as sense and reason would have made it, even if this vision was sometimes distorted by personal unhappiness and by the rage of despair. The more important elements in Swift's creativity belong to his prose writings, but they are to be found to some extent in his verse too. His hatred of dishonest speech and writing, for instance, is expressed not only destructively in *Polite Conversation* and *A Description of the Morning*; it is to be found expressed positively, throughout his poems, in a relish for the honest and salty speech of comparatively humble people. Swift's delight in this kind of speech is nowhere better revealed than in the exquisite *Frances Harris's Petition* in which also Swift's essential humanity shines without distortion. This is a masterpiece, wholly original, not less moving because it is also comic. Here Swift writes with the observation and affection, not without a hint of mockery, of one who loves real people, however much his misanthropy embitters him against the false and the powerful.

It is all very well for critics to speak of such things as 'prose trifles'. Exalted, impassioned, they may not be; but they are poetic in a quite precise and real sense. They are poetic in a way which would have appealed even to the arch-Romantic, Wordsworth, for they are written 'in a selection of the language really used by men'. Swift had, among other gifts, an ear unerringly responsive to natural, unaffected and racy language: in selecting such language for his verse he made not only an aesthetic but also a moral judgement, applauding truth and honesty and by implication condemning falsehood and artificiality. It is as if he said to the polite reading public, 'You may prefer the style of the Strephons and Phyllises of neo-pastoral poems; I prefer the style of Mrs. Harris and Mary the Cook-Maid.'

The Augustan age was not on the whole much to be commended on its attitude to women. In prose Defoe was conspicuous for his humanity in his portraits of women of a certain class, and he was in advance of his age in his advocacy of education for girls. But the accepted attitude among polite verse-writers was a combination of gallantry, in the French sense, and indulgent condescension. Swift went further than any poet in exposing conventional views of women; but in his touching and beautiful birthday verses to Stella he combines tenderness and good sense with a real and unaffected regard for her true qualities. His last birthday poem to her, written in 1727, less than a year before her death, expresses morality without priggishness, love without illusion.

Swift's poems have been underrated for several interesting and connected reasons. First, they are of course overshadowed by his much greater prose satires. The author of *Gulliver* and *A Modest Proposal* is indisputably pre-eminent in his field. Nevertheless, if Swift had not written his prose satires, his reputation as a poet would almost certainly stand higher. He was also overshadowed by his younger contemporary, Pope. Literary historians like neat arrangements, and have been content to label Swift and Pope as the greatest prose and verse satirists of their age respectively.

Another cause of the neglect of Swift's poems is that he never set himself up as a professional poet. He was unwilling to publish them under his own name, partly for fear of political reprisal. He received no money for his poems, and no collected edition appeared until he was an old man.

Nineteenth-century critics were repelled by the brutality and coarseness of much of Swift's verse, and this helped to keep it in obscurity until recent times. Literary critics have, on the whole, been content to treat Swift as a prose satirist. But there is another, simpler reason for their inattention to his poems. The matter was expressed with characteristic dry clarity by Dr. Johnson, who himself had not much to say about them:

In the Poetical Works of Dr. Swift there is not much upon which the critick can exercise his powers. They are often humorous, almost always light, and have the qualities which recommend such compositions, easiness and gaiety. They are, for the most part, what their author intended. The diction is correct, the numbers are smooth, and the rhymes exact. There seldom occurs a hard-laboured expression or a redundant epithet; all his verses exemplify his own definition of a good style, they consist of *proper words in proper places.*

It was said . . . that Swift had never been known to take a single

13

thought from any writer, ancient or modern. This is not literally true; but perhaps no writer can easily be found that has borrowed so little, or that in all his excellences and all his defects has so well maintained his claim to be considered as original.

The fact, however, that there is not much for conventional criticism to say about these poems is no reason for neglecting them. On the contrary, there is every reason why readers of poetry should enjoy them, quite simply and without difficulty, for the very qualities which make them unacceptable to a certain type of critic. In the first place, they are, as Johnson saw, highly original. In style they owed something to Butler, but they owe little to him directly, and far outdo *Hudibras* in ease, naturalness and variety. In the second place, many of them are unaffectedly amusing. Swift preferred humour to wit, and he is never merely clever. His poems are not adorned with gems of expression inviting admiration. The style never draws attention to itself and is accordingly the more effective. We are always interested in what Swift says, never distracted by the way in which he says it. This of course is, paradoxically, due to the excellence of his style. At their best his poems are almost daring in their naturalness, their simplicity and their clarity. 'They are ... what their author intended.' For these reasons his verse reads aloud admirably. The ear is always satisfied, never glutted.

The style is the man, and Swift, for all the complications of his nature, its contradictions and contrariety, was a plain man. He hated affectation, insincerity, obsequiousness, as well as injustice and corruption. That he had learned to hate them the hardest way, by being their victim, strengthens his passion and conviction. It is impossible to say what manner of man he would have been had he not been the victim of injustice from childhood. Yet it is impossible to believe that he would not have possessed in all circumstances the virtues of plainness, directness, honesty and truthfulness. That these virtues, translated into language, are the virtues of prose does not mean that they are out of place in poetry. If through mistakenly looking in Swift for the qualities we associate with Donne, Marvell, Blake, Wordsworth or Keats we fail to recognize his positive

14

qualities, we miss something unique and valuable in English poetry. When we are in the mood to 'place' poets in order of merit—a mistaken but understandable weakness—we will not often place Swift among the highest. But when we are in the mood simply to read poems for their immediate effectiveness and are looking for something different from the sexual raptures of Donne, the epigrammatic glitter of Pope, the lyric intensity of Blake, the rhetoric of Byron, the introspection of Coleridge, the nature-worship of Wordsworth—if we are prepared to admit that poetry has other provinces, then we may turn to Swift with enjoyment, even relief. He had little sense of the bardic vocation. He wrote not for any self-regarding motive, worthy or unworthy; he wrote to entertain his friends, to castigate his enemies or to further a cause. He wrote in an anti-poetic age, when *vers de société* of one kind or another was the best that could be achieved. Fanaticism, 'enthusiasm' and mysticism were out; good sense, reason and sobriety were in. The nation had been almost ruined by the madness of political and religious fanatics: true poetry was one of the first casualties. Arnold's summing-up of the age as one of 'prose and reason' has come in for some hard knocks, but it remains essentially true. The poetry of the time rarely gets off the ground: but if good sense is not altogether fatal to poetry, if truth will serve as a Muse, if humanity, humour, originality and perspicuity can be found in poetry, Swift was a true poet. Nor would it be right to insist too exclusively on his good sense. He was a passionate, as well as a plain man; and he is often at his most effective and moving when he throws aside humour, good sense and prudence, and lashes out with merciless directness at a vicious politician, an oppressive landlord, or a sycophantic churchman. The wholeness, the many-sidedness of the man revealed in Swift's poems has not been fully appreciated. The violent, corrosive misanthrope is only the dark obverse of the warm and large-hearted humanitarian who dwelt lovingly on the salt speech of ordinary Dubliners and composed verses for street vendors.

The text of the poems is reprinted from *The Poems of Jonathan*

Swift, edited by Harold Williams (second edition 1958), by permission of the Clarendon Press, Oxford.

For help with the present volume at the proof stage I am indebted to Reg Mutter of the University of Sussex, who offered many valuable suggestions and put me right over a number of points of fact and interpretation. For any remaining errors, however, I am solely responsible.

J. R.

Lewes, 1966.

SELECT BIBLIOGRAPHY

Prose and Poetry

Swift: The Prose Works, edited by H. Davis, Oxford, 1939–
The Correspondence of Jonathan Swift, edited by H. Williams, Oxford, 5 volumes, 1963–65.
Journal to Stella, edited by H. Williams, Oxford, 2 volumes, 1948.
The Poems of Jonathan Swift, edited by H. Williams, Oxford, 3 volumes, 1937.

Biography and Criticism

Ricardo Quintana, *Swift: An Introduction*, Oxford, 1954.
R. C. Churchill, *He Served Human Liberty: An Essay on the Genius of Jonathan Swift*, London, 1946.
J. M. Murry, *Swift: A Critical Biography*, London, 1954.
Irvin Ehrenpreis, *Swift: The Man, His Works and the Age. Vol. I, Mr. Swift and his Contemporaries*, London, 1962.
Nigel Dennis, *Jonathan Swift*, London, 1965.

Verses Wrote in a Lady's Ivory Table-Book

PERUSE my Leaves thro' ev'ry Part,
And think thou seest my owners Heart,
Scrawl'd o'er with Trifles thus, and quite
As hard, as sensless, and as light:
Expos'd to every Coxcomb's Eyes,
But hid with Caution from the Wise.
Here you may read (*Dear Charming Saint*)
Beneath (*A new Receit for Paint*)
Here in Beau-spelling (*tru tel deth*)
There in her own (*far an el breth*)   10
Here (*lovely Nymph pronounce my doom*)
There (*A safe way to use Perfume*)
Here, a Page fill'd with Billet Doux;
On t'other side (*laid out for Shoes*)
(*Madam, I dye without your Grace*)
(*Item, for half a Yard of Lace.*)
Who that had Wit would place it here,
For every peeping Fop to Jear.
To think that your Brains Issue is
Expos'd to th' Excrement of his,   20
In power of Spittle and a Clout
When e're he please to blot it out;
And then to heighten the Disgrace
Clap his own Nonsence in the place.
Whoe're expects to hold his part
In such a Book and such a Heart,
If he be Wealthy and a Fool
Is in all Points the fittest Tool,
Of whom it may be justly said,
He's a Gold Pencil tipt with Lead.   30

Frances Harris's Petition

TO THEIR EXCELLENCIES THE LORDS
JUSTICES OF IRELAND.

The Humble Petition of Frances Harris,
Who must Starve, and Die a Maid if it miscarries.

Humbly Sheweth.

THAT I went to warm my self in Lady *Betty*'s Chamber, because I
was cold,

And I had in a Purse, seven Pound, four Shillings and six Pence,
besides Farthings, in Money, and Gold;

So because I had been buying things for my *Lady* last Night,

I was resolved to tell my Money, to see if it was right:

Now you must know, because my Trunk has a very bad Lock,

Therefore all the Money, I have, which, *God* knows, is a very
small Stock,

I keep in a Pocket ty'd about my Middle, next my Smock.

So when I went to put up my Purse, as *God* would have it, my
Smock was unript,

And, instead of putting it into my Pocket, down it slipt:

Then the Bell rung, and I went down to put my *Lady* to Bed,   10

And, *God* knows, I thought my Money was as safe as my Maiden-
head.

So when I came up again, I found my Pocket feel very light,

But when I search'd, and miss'd my Purse, *Lord*! I thought I should
have sunk outright:

Lord! Madam, says *Mary*, how d'ye do? Indeed, says I, never worse;

But pray, *Mary*, can you tell what I have done with my Purse!

Lord help me, said *Mary*, I never stirr'd out of this Place!

Nay, said I, I had it in Lady *Betty's* Chamber, that's a plain Case.

So *Mary* got me to Bed, and cover'd me up warm,

However, she stole away my Garters, that I might do my self no Harm:

So I tumbl'd and toss'd all Night, as you may very well think,   20

But hardly ever set my Eyes together, or slept a Wink.

So I was a-dream'd, methought, that we went and search'd the Folks round,

And in a Corner of Mrs. *Dukes's* Box, ty'd in a Rag, the Money was found.

So next Morning we told *Whittle*, and he fell a Swearing;

Then my Dame *Wadgar* came, and she, you know, is thick of Hearing;

Dame, said I, as loud as I could bawl, do you know what a Loss I have had?

Nay, said she, my Lord *Collway's* Folks are all very sad,

For my Lord *Dromedary* comes a *Tuesday* without fail;

Pugh! said I, but that's not the Business that I ail.

Says *Cary*, says he, I have been a Servant this Five and Twenty Years, come Spring,   30

And in all the Places I liv'd, I never heard of such a Thing.

Yes, says the *Steward*, I remember when I was at my Lady *Shrewsbury's*,

Such a thing as this happen'd, just about the time of *Goosberries*.

So I went to the Party suspected, and I found her full of Grief;

(Now you must know, of all Things in the World, I hate a Thief.)

However, I was resolv'd to bring the Discourse slily about,

Mrs. *Dukes*, said I, here's an ugly Accident has happen'd out;

'Tis not that I value the Money three Skips of a Louse;

But the Thing I stand upon, is the Credit of the House;

'Tis true, seven Pound, four Shillings, and six Pence, makes a great Hole in my Wages,   40

Besides, as they say, Service is no Inheritance in these Ages.

Now, Mrs. *Dukes*, you know, and every Body understands,

That tho' 'tis hard to judge, yet Money can't go without Hands.
The *Devil* take me, said she, (blessing her self,) if I ever saw't!
So she roar'd like a *Bedlam*, as tho' I had call'd her all to naught;
So you know, what could I say to her any more,
I e'en left her, and came away as wise as I was before.
Well: But then they would have had me gone to the Cunning
    Man;
No, said I, 'tis the same Thing, the *Chaplain* will be here anon.
So the *Chaplain* came in; now the Servants say, he is my Sweet-
    heart, 50
Because he's always in my Chamber, and I always take his Part;
So, as the *Devil* would have it, before I was aware, out I blunder'd,
Parson, said I, can you cast a *Nativity*, when a Body's plunder'd?
(Now you must know, he hates to be call'd *Parson*, like the *Devil*.)
Truly, says he, Mrs. *Nab*, it might become you to be more civil:
If your Money be gone, as a Learned *Divine* says, d'ye see,
You are no *Text* for my Handling, so take that from me:
I was never taken for a *Conjurer* before, I'd have you to know.
Lord, said I, don't be angry, I'm sure I never thought you so;
You know, I honour the Cloth, I design to be a *Parson's* Wife, 60
I never took one in *Your Coat* for a *Conjurer* in all my life.
With that, he twisted his Girdle at me like a Rope, as who should
    say,
Now you may go hang your self for me, and so went away.
Well; I thought I should have swoon'd; *Lord*, said I, what shall
    I do?
I have lost my *Money*, and shall lose my *True-Love* too.
Then my *Lord* call'd me; *Harry*, said my *Lord*, don't cry,
I'll give something towards thy Loss; and says my *Lady*, so will I.
Oh but, said I, what if after all my Chaplain won't *come to*?
For that, he said, (an't please your *Excellencies*) I must Petition You.

The Premises tenderly consider'd, I desire your *Excellencies* Pro-
    tection, 70
And that I may have a Share in next *Sunday's* Collection:

And over and above, that I may have your *Excellencies* Letter,
With an Order for the *Chaplain* aforesaid; or instead of Him, a
    Better:
And then your poor *Petitioner*, both Night and Day,
Or the *Chaplain*, (for 'tis his *Trade*) as in Duty bound, shall ever
    Pray.

A Ballad on the Game of Traffick

My *Lord* to find out who must deal
    Delivers Cards about,
But the first Knave does seldom fail
    To find the *Doctor* out.

But then his *Honour* cry'd, Godzooks!
    And seem'd to knit his Brow;
For on a Knave he never looks
    But H' thinks upon *Jack How*.

My *Lady* tho' she is no Player
    Some bungling Partner takes,   10
And wedg'd in Corner of a Chair
    Takes Snuff, and holds the Stakes.

Dame *Floyd* looks out in grave Suspence
    For Pair-royals and Sequents;
But wisely cautious of her Pence,
    The Castle seldom frequents.

23

Quoth *Herries*, fairly putting Cases,
 I'd won it on my Word,
If I had but a Pair of Aces,
 And could pick up a Third.   20

But *Weston* has a new-cast Gown
 On *Sundays* to be fine in,
And if she can but win a *Crown*,
 'Twill just new dye the Lining.

"With these is Parson *Swift*,
 "Not knowing how to spend his Time,
"Does make a wretched Shift,
 "To deafen 'em with Puns and Rhime.

A Description of the Morning

Now hardly here and there an Hackney-Coach
Appearing, show'd the Ruddy Morns Approach.
Now *Betty* from her Masters Bed had flown,
And softly stole to discompose her own.
The Slipshod Prentice from his Masters Door,
Had par'd the Dirt, and Sprinkled round the Floor.
Now *Moll* had whirl'd her Mop with dext'rous Airs,
Prepar'd to Scrub the Entry and the Stairs.
The Youth with Broomy Stumps began to trace
The Kennel-Edge, where Wheels had worn the Place.   10
The Smallcoal-Man was heard with Cadence deep,
'Till drown'd in Shriller Notes of Chimney-Sweep,
Duns at his Lordships Gate began to meet,
And Brickdust *Moll* had Scream'd through half the Street.

The Turnkey now his Flock returning sees,
Duly let out a Nights to Steal for Fees.
The watchful Bailiffs take their silent Stands,
And School-Boys lag with Satchels in their Hands.

A Description of a City Shower

CAREFUL Observers may fortel the Hour
(By sure Prognosticks) when to dread a Show'r:
While Rain depends, the pensive Cat gives o'er
Her Frolicks, and pursues her Tail no more.
Returning Home at Night, you'll find the Sink
Strike your offended Sense with double Stink.
If you be wise, then go not far to Dine,
You'll spend in Coach-hire more than save in Wine.
A coming Show'r your shooting Corns presage,
Old Aches throb, your hollow Tooth will rage.   10
Sauntring in Coffee-house is *Dulman* seen;
He damns the Climate, and complains of Spleen.

MEAN while the South rising with dabbled Wings,
A Sable Cloud a-thwart the Welkin flings,
That swill'd more Liquor than it could contain,
And like a Drunkard gives it up again.
Brisk *Susan* whips her Linen from the Rope,
While the first drizzling Show'r is born aslope,
Such is that Sprinkling which some careless Quean
Flirts on you from her Mop, but not so clean.   20
You fly, invoke the Gods; then turning, stop
To rail; she singing, still whirls on her Mop.
Not yet, the Dust had shun'd th' unequal Strife,
But aided by the Wind, fought still for Life;

And wafted with its Foe by violent Gust,
'Twas doubtful which was Rain, and which was Dust.
Ah! where must needy Poet seek for Aid,
When Dust and Rain at once his Coat invade;
His only Coat, where Dust confus'd with Rain,
Roughen the Nap, and leave a mingled Stain.   30

NOW in contiguous Drops the Flood comes down,
Threat'ning with Deluge this *Devoted* Town.
To Shops in Crouds the daggled Females fly,
Pretend to cheapen Goods, but nothing buy.
The Templer spruce, while ev'ry Spout's a-broach,
Stays till 'tis fair, yet seems to call a Coach.
The tuck'd-up Sempstress walks with hasty Strides,
While Streams run down her oil'd Umbrella's Sides.
Here various Kinds by various Fortunes led,
Commence Acquaintance underneath a Shed.   40
Triumphant Tories, and desponding Whigs,
Forget their Fewds, and join to save their Wigs,
Box'd in a Chair the Beau impatient sits,
While Spouts run clatt'ring o'er the Roof by Fits;
And ever and anon with frightful Din
The Leather sounds, he trembles from within.
So when *Troy* Chair-men bore the Wooden Steed,
Pregnant with *Greeks*, impatient to be freed,
(Those Bully *Greeks*, who, as the Moderns do,
Instead of paying Chair-men, run them thro'.)   50
Laoco'n struck the Outside with his Spear,
And each imprison'd Hero quak'd for Fear.

NOW from all Parts the swelling Kennels flow,
And bear their Trophies with them as they go:
Filth of all Hues and Odours seem to tell
What Street they sail'd from, by their Sight and Smell.
They, as each Torrent drives, with rapid Force
From *Smithfield*, or St. *Pulchre*'s shape their Course,

And in huge Confluent join at *Snow-Hill* Ridge,
Fall from the *Conduit* prone to *Holborn-Bridge*.   60
Sweepings from Butchers Stalls, Dung, Guts, and Blood,
Drown'd Puppies, stinking Sprats, all drench'd in Mud,
Dead Cats and Turnip-Tops come tumbling down the
    Flood.

Cadenus and Vanessa

THE *Shepherds* and the *Nymphs* were seen
Pleading before the *Cyprian* Queen.
The Council for the Fair began,
Accusing that false Creature, *Man.*

The Brief with weighty Crimes was charg'd,
On which the Pleader much enlarg'd;
That *Cupid* now has lost his Art,
Or blunts the Point of ev'ry Dart;
His Altar now no longer smokes,
His Mother's Aid no Youth invokes: 10
This tempts Free-thinkers to refine,
And bring in doubt their Pow'r divine;
Now Love is dwindled to Intrigue,
And Marriage grown a Money-League.
Which Crimes aforesaid (with her Leave)
Were (as he humbly did conceive)
Against our Sov'reign Lady's Peace,
Against the Statutes in that Case,
Against her Dignity and Crown:
Then pray'd an Answer, and sat down.   20

The *Nymphs* with Scorn beheld their Foes:
When the Defendant's Council rose,

And, what no Lawyer ever lack'd,
With Impudence own'd all the Fact.
But, what the gentlest Heart would vex,
Laid all the Fault on t'other Sex.
That modern Love is no such Thing
As what those antient Poets sing;
A Fire celestial, chaste, refin'd,
Conceiv'd and kindled in the Mind, 30
Which having found an equal Flame,
Unites, and both become the same,
In different Breasts together burn,
Together both to Ashes turn.
But Women now feel no such Fire,
And only know the gross Desire;
Their Passions move in lower Spheres,
Where-e'er Caprice or Folly steers.
A Dog, a Parrot, or an Ape,
Or some worse Brute in human Shape, 40
Engross the Fancies of the Fair,
The few soft Moments they can spare,
From Visits to receive and pay,
From Scandal, Politicks, and Play,
From Fans, and Flounces, and Brocades,
From Equipage and Park-Parades,
From all the thousand Female Toys,
From every Trifle that employs
The out or inside of their Heads,
Between their Toylets and their Beds. 50

In a dull Stream, which moving slow
You hardly see the Current flow,
If a small Breeze obstructs the Course,
It whirls about for Want of Force,
And as its narrow Circle gathers
Nothing but Chaff, and Straws, and Feathers:

The Current of a Female Mind
Stops thus, and turns with ev'ry Wind;
Thus whirling round, together draws
Fools, Fops, and Rakes, for Chaff and Straws.   60
Hence we conclude, no Women's Hearts
Are won by Virtue, Wit, and Parts;
Nor are the Men of Sense to blame,
For Breasts incapable of Flame;
The Fault must on the *Nymphs* be plac'd,
Grown so corrupted in their Taste.

The Pleader having spoke his best,
Had Witness ready to attest,
Who fairly could on Oath depose,
When Questions on the Fact arose,   70
That ev'ry Article was true;
Nor further those Deponents knew:
Therefore he humbly would insist,
The Bill might be with Costs dismist.

The Cause appear'd of so much Weight,
That *Venus*, from the Judgment-Seat,
Desir'd them not to talk so loud,
Else she must interpose a Cloud:
For if the Heav'nly Folk should know
These Pleadings in the Courts below,   80
That Mortals here disdain to love;
She ne'er could shew her Face above.
For Gods, their Betters, are too wise
To value that which Men despise.
And then, said she, my Son and I
Must strole in Air 'twixt Earth and Sky;
Or else, shut out from Heaven and Earth,
Fly to the Sea, my Place of Birth;
There live with daggl'd *Mermaids* pent,
And keep on Fish perpetual *Lent*.   90

But since the Case appear'd so nice,
She thought it best to take Advice.
The *Muses*, by their King's Permission,
Tho' Foes to Love, attend the Session,
And on the Right Hand took their Places
In Order; on the Left, the *Graces:*
To whom she might her Doubts propose
On all Emergencies that rose.
The *Muses* oft were seen to frown;
The *Graces* half asham'd look'd down;   100
And 'twas observ'd, there were but few
Of either Sex, among the Crew,
Whom she or her Assessors knew.
The Goddess soon began to see
Things were not ripe for a Decree,
And said she must consult her Books,
The *Lovers Fleta's, Bractons, Cokes.*
First to a dapper Clerk she beckon'd,
To turn to *Ovid*, Book the Second;
She then referr'd them to a Place   110
In *Virgil (vide Dido*'s Case:)
As for *Tibullus*'s Reports,
They never pass'd for Law in Courts;
For *Cowley*'s Briefs, and Pleas of *Waller*,
Still their Authority was smaller.

There was on both Sides much to say:
She'd hear the Cause another Day,
And so she did, and then a Third,
She heard it—there she kept her Word;
But with Rejoinders and Replies,   120
Long Bills, and Answers, stuff'd with Lies,
Demur, Imparlance, and Essoign,
The Parties ne'er could Issue join:

For Sixteen Years the Cause was spun,
And then stood where it first begun.

Now, gentle *Clio*, sing or say,
What *Venus* meant by this Delay.
The Goddess much perplex'd in Mind,
To see her Empire thus declin'd,
When first this grand Debate arose   130
Above her Wisdom to compose,
Conceiv'd a Project in her Head,
To work her Ends; which if it sped,
Wou'd shew the Merits of the Cause,
Far better than consulting Laws.

In a glad Hour *Lucina*'s Aid
Produc'd on Earth a wond'rous Maid,
On whom the Queen of Love was bent
To try a new Experiment:
She threw her Law-books on the Shelf,   140
And thus debated with herself.

Since Men alledge they ne'er can find
Those Beauties in a Female Mind,
Which raise a Flame that will endure
For ever, uncorrupt and pure;
If 'tis with Reason they complain,
This Infant shall restore my Reign.
I'll search where ev'ry Virtue dwells,
From Courts inclusive, down to Cells,
What Preachers talk, or Sages write,   150
These I will gather and unite,
And represent them to Mankind
Collected in that Infant's Mind.

This said, she plucks in Heav'ns high Bow'rs
A Sprig of *Amaranthine* Flow'rs,

In Nectar thrice infuses Bays,
Three times refin'd in *Titan*'s Rays:
Then calls the *Graces* to her Aid,
And sprinkles thrice the new-born Maid.
From whence the tender Skin assumes   160
A Sweetness above all Perfumes;
From whence a Cleanliness remains,
Incapable of outward Stains;
From whence that Decency of Mind,
So lovely in the Female Kind,
Where not one careless Thought intrudes,
Less modest than the Speech of Prudes;
Where never Blush was call'd in Aid,
That spurious Virtue in a Maid,
A Virtue but at second-hand;   170
They blush because they understand.

The *Graces* next wou'd act their Part,
And shew'd but little of their Art;
Their Work was half already done,
The Child with native Beauty shone,
The outward Form no Help requir'd:
Each breathing on her thrice, inspir'd
That gentle, soft, engaging Air,
Which in old Times adorn'd the Fair;
And said, '*Vanessa* be the Name,   180
"By which thou shalt be known to Fame:
"*Vanessa*, by the Gods enroll'd:
"Her Name on Earth——shall not be told."

But still the Work was not compleat,
When *Venus* thought on a Deceit:
Drawn by her Doves, away she flies,
And finds out *Pallas* in the Skies:
Dear *Pallas*, I have been this Morn
To see a lovely infant born:

A Boy in yonder Isle below,   190
So like my own, without his Bow,
By Beauty cou'd your Heart be won,
You'd swear it is *Apollo*'s Son;
But it shall ne'er be said, a Child
So hopeful, has by me been spoil'd;
I have enough besides to spare,
And give him wholly to your Care.

　Wisdom's above suspecting Wiles:
The Queen of Learning gravely smiles,
Down from *Olympus* comes with Joy,   200
Mistakes *Vanessa* for a Boy;
Then sows within her tender Mind
Seeds long unknown to Womankind,
For manly Bosoms chiefly fit,
The Seeds of Knowledge, Judgment, Wit.
Her Soul was suddenly endu'd
With Justice, Truth and Fortitude;
With Honour, which no Breath can Stain,
Which Malice must attack in vain;
With open Heart and bounteous Hand: 210
But *Pallas* here was at a Stand;
She knew in our degen'rate Days
Bare Virtue could not live on Praise,
That Meat must be with Money bought;
She therefore, upon second Thought,
Infus'd, yet as it were by Stealth,
Some small Regard for State and Wealth:
Of which, as she grew up, there stay'd
A Tincture in the prudent Maid:
She manag'd her Estate with Care,   220
Yet lik'd three Footmen to her Chair.
But lest he shou'd neglect his Studies
Like a young Heir, the thrifty Goddess

33

(For fear young Master shou'd be spoil'd,)
Wou'd use him like a younger Child;
And, after long computing, found
'Twou'd come to just Five Thousand Pound.

The Queen of Love was pleas'd, and proud,
To see *Vanessa* thus endow'd;
She doubted not but such a Dame   230
Thro' ev'ry Breast wou'd dart a Flame;
That ev'ry rich and lordly Swain
With Pride wou'd drag about her Chain;
That Scholars wou'd forsake their Books
To study bright *Vanessa's* Looks:
As she advanc'd, that Womankind
Wou'd by her Model form their Mind,
And all their Conduct wou'd be try'd
By her, as an unerring Guide.
Offending Daughters oft wou'd hear   240
Vanessa's Praise rung in their Ear:
Miss *Betty*, when she does a Fault,
Lets fall her Knife, or spills the Salt,
Will thus be by her Mother chid,
"Tis what *Vanessa* never did."
Thus by the Nymphs and Swains ador'd,
My Pow'r shall be again restor'd,
And happy Lovers bless my Reign——
So *Venus* hop'd, but hop'd in vain.

For when in time the *Martial Maid*   250
Found out the Trick that *Venus* play'd,
She shakes her Helm, she knits her Brows,
And fir'd with Indignation vows,
To-morrow, ere the setting Sun,
She'd all undo, that she had done.

But in the Poets we may find,
A wholesome Law, Time out of mind,
Had been confirm'd by Fate's Decree;
That Gods, of whatso'er Degree,
Resume not what themselves have giv'n,   260
Or any Brother-God in Heav'n:
Which keeps the Peace among the Gods,
Or they must always be at Odds.
And *Pallas*, if she broke the Laws,
Must yield her Foe the stronger Cause;
A Shame to one so much ador'd
For Wisdom, at *Jove's* Council-Board.
Besides, she fear'd the Queen of Love
Wou'd meet with better Friends above.
And tho' she must with Grief reflect,   270
To see a Mortal Virgin deck'd
With Graces, hitherto unknown
To Female Breasts, except her own;
Yet she wou'd act as best became
A Goddess of unspotted Fame:
She knew, by Augury Divine,
Venus wou'd fail in her Design:
She study'd well the Point, and found
Her Foe's Conclusions were not sound,
From Premisses erroneous brought,   280
And therefore the Deductions nought,
And must have contrary Effects
To what her treach'rous Foe expects.

In proper Season *Pallas* meets
The Queen of Love, whom thus she greets,
(For Gods, we are by *Homer* told,
Can in Celestial Language scold)
Perfidious Goddess! but in vain
You form'd this Project in your Brain,

A Project for thy Talents fit, 290
With much Deceit and little Wit;
Thou hast, as thou shalt quickly see,
Deceiv'd thy self, instead of me;
For how can Heav'nly Wisdom prove
An Instrument to earthly Love?
Know'st thou not yet that Men commence
Thy Votaries, for Want of Sense?
Nor shall *Vanessa* be the Theme
To manage thy abortive Scheme;
She'll prove the greatest of thy Foes: 300
And yet I scorn to interpose,
But using neither Skill, nor Force,
Leave all Things to their Nat'ral Course.

The Goddess thus pronounc'd her Doom:
When, lo! *Vanessa* in her Bloom,
Advanc'd like *Atalanta*'s Star,
But rarely seen, and seen from far:
In a new World with Caution stept,
Watch'd all the Company she kept,
Well knowing from the Books she read 310
What dangerous Paths young Virgins tread;
Wou'd seldom at the Park appear,
Nor saw the Play-House twice a Year;
Yet not incurious, was inclin'd
To know the Converse of Mankind.

First issu'd from Perfumers Shops
A Croud of fashionable Fops;
They ask'd her, how she lik'd the Play,
Then told the Tattle of the Day,
A Duel fought last Night at Two, 320
About a Lady——You know who;
Mention'd a new *Italian*, come
Either from *Muscovy* or *Rome*;

Gave Hints of who and who's together;
Then fell to talking of the Weather:
Last Night was so extremely fine,
The Ladies walk'd till after Nine.
Then in soft Voice and Speech absurd,
With Nonsense ev'ry second Word,
With Fustian from exploded Plays,   330
They celebrate her Beauty's Praise,
Run o'er their Cant of stupid Lies,
And tell the Murders of her Eyes.

With silent Scorn *Vanessa* sat,
Scarce list'ning to their idle Chat;
Further than sometimes by a Frown,
When they grew pert, to pull them down.
At last she spitefully was bent
To try their Wisdom's full Extent;
And said, she valu'd nothing less   340
Than Titles, Figure, Shape, and Dress;
That, Merit should be chiefly plac'd
In Judgment, Knowledge, Wit, and Taste;
And these, she offer'd to dispute,
Alone distinguish'd Man from Brute:
That, present Times have no Pretence
To Virtue, in the Noblest Sense,
By *Greeks* and *Romans* understood,
To perish for our Country's Good.
She nam'd the antient Heroes round,   350
Explain'd for what they were renown'd;
Then spoke with Censure, or Applause,
Of foreign Customs, Rites, and Laws;
Thro' Nature, and thro' Art she rang'd,
And gracefully her Subject chang'd:
In vain: her Hearers had no Share
In all she spoke, except to stare.

Their Judgment was upon the Whole,
—That Lady is the dullest Soul—
Then tipt their Forehead in a Jeer,   360
As who should say—she wants it here;
She may be handsome, young and rich,
But none will burn her for a Witch.

      A Party next of glitt'ring Dames,
From round the Purlieus of *St. James*,
Came early, out of pure Good-will,
To see the Girl in Deshabille.
Their Clamour 'lighting from their Chairs,
Grew louder, all the Way up Stairs;
At Entrance loudest, where they found   370
The Room with Volumes litter'd round
Vanessa held *Montaigne*, and read,
Whilst Mrs. *Susan* comb'd her Head:
They call'd for Tea and Chocolate,
And fell into their usual Chat,
Discoursing with important Face,
On Ribbons, Fans, and Gloves and Lace;
Shew'd Patterns just from *India* brought,
And gravely ask'd her what she thought,
Whether the Red or Green were best,   380
And what they cost? *Vanessa* guess'd,
As came into her Fancy first,
Nam'd half the Rates, and lik'd the worst.
To Scandal next——What aukward Thing
Was that, last *Sunday* in the Ring?
——I'm sorry *Mopsa* breaks so fast;
I said her Face would never last.
Corinna with that youthful Air,
Is thirty, and a Bit to spare.
Her Fondness for a certain Earl   390
Began, when I was but a Girl.

Phyllis, who but a Month ago
Was marry'd to the *Tunbridge* Beau,
I saw coquetting t'other Night
In publick with that odious Knight.

They railly'd next *Vanessa*'s Dress;
That Gown was made for Old Queen *Bess*.
Dear Madam, Let me set your Head:
Don't you intend to put on Red?
A Pettycoat without a Hoop!   400
Sure, you are not asham'd to stoop;
With handsome Garters at your Knees,
No matter what a Fellow sees.

Fill'd with Disdain, with Rage inflam'd,
Both of her self and Sex asham'd,
The Nymph stood silent out of spight,
Nor wou'd vouchsafe to set them right.
Away the fair Detractors went,
And gave, by turns, their Censures Vent.
She's not so handsome, in my Eyes: 410
For Wit, I wonder where it lies.
She's fair and clean, and that's the most;
But why proclaim her for a Toast?
A Baby Face, no Life, no Airs,
But what she learnt at Country Fairs;
Scarce knows what Diff'rence is between
Rich *Flanders* Lace, and Colberteen.
I'll undertake my little *Nancy*
In Flounces has a better Fancy.
With all her Wit, I wou'd not ask   420
Her Judgment, how to buy a Mask.
We begg'd her but to patch her Face,
She never hit one proper Place;
Which every Girl at five Years old
Can do as soon as she is told.

I own, that out-of-fashion Stuff
Becomes the *Creature* well enough.
The Girl might pass, if we cou'd get her
To know the World a little better.
(*To know the World*! a modern Phrase,   430
For Visits, Ombre, Balls and Plays.)

   Thus, to the World's perpetual Shame,
The *Queen of Beauty* lost her Aim.
Too late with Grief she understood,
Pallas had done more Harm than Good;
For great Examples are but vain,
Where Ignorance begets Disdain.
Both Sexes, arm'd with Guilt and Spite,
Against *Vanessa*'s Pow'r unite;
To copy her, few Nymphs aspir'd;   440
Her Virtues fewer Swains admir'd:
So Stars beyond a certain Height
Give Mortals neither Heat nor Light.

   Yet some of either Sex, endow'd
With Gifts superior to the Crowd,
With Virtue, Knowledge, Taste and Wit,
She condescended to admit:
With pleasing Arts she could reduce
Mens Talents to their proper Use;
And with Address each Genius held   450
To that wherein it most excell'd;
Thus making others Wisdom known,
Cou'd please them, and improve her own.
A modest Youth said something new,
She plac'd it in the strongest View.
All humble Worth she strove to raise;
Would not be prais'd, yet lov'd to praise.
The Learned met with free Approach,
Although they came not in a Coach.

Some Clergy too she wou'd allow,   460
Nor quarrell'd at their aukward Bow.
But this was for *Cadenus'* sake;
A Gownman of a diff'rent Make.
Whom *Pallas*, once *Vanessa*'s Tutor,
Had fix'd on for her Coadjutor.

But *Cupid*, full of Mischief, longs
To vindicate his Mother's Wrongs.
On *Pallas* all Attempts are vain;
One way he knows to give her Pain:
Vows, on *Vanessa*'s Heart to take   470
Due Vengeance, for her Patron's sake.
Those early Seeds by *Venus* sown,
In spight of *Pallas*, now were grown;
And *Cupid* hop'd they wou'd improve
By Time, and ripen into Love.
The Boy made use of all his Craft,
In vain discharging many a Shaft,
Pointed at Col'nels, Lords, and Beaux;
Cadenus warded off the Blows:
For placing still some Book betwixt,   480
The Darts were in the Cover fix'd,
Or often blunted and recoil'd,
On *Plutarch*'s Morals struck, were spoil'd.

The Queen of Wisdom cou'd foresee,
But not prevent the Fates decree;
And human Caution tries in vain
To break that Adamantine Chain.
Vanessa, tho' by *Pallas* taught,
By *Love* invulnerable thought,
Searching in Books for Wisdom's Aid,   490
Was, in the very Search, betray'd.

Cupid, tho' all his Darts were lost,
Yet still resolv'd to spare no Cost;
He could not answer to his Fame
The Triumphs of that stubborn Dame,
A Nymph so hard to be subdu'd,
Who neither was Coquette nor Prude.
I find, says he, she wants a Doctor,
Both to adore her and instruct her;
I'll give her what she most admires,   500
Among those venerable Sires.
Cadenus is a Subject fit,
Grown old in Politicks and Wit;
Caress'd by Ministers of State,
Of half Mankind the Dread and Hate.
Whate'er Vexations Love attend,
She need no Rivals apprehend.
Her Sex, with universal Voice,
Must laugh at her capricious Choice.

Cadenus many things had writ;   510
Vanessa much esteem'd his Wit,
And call'd for his Poetick Works;
Mean time the Boy in secret lurks,
And while the Book was in her Hand,
The Urchin from his private Stand
Took Aim, and shot with all his Strength
A Dart of such prodigious Length,
It pierc'd the feeble Volume thro',
And deep transfix'd her Bosom too.
Some Lines, more moving than the rest,   520
Stuck to the Point that pierc'd her Breast;
And, born directly to the Heart,
With Pains unknown increas'd her Smart.

Vanessa, not in Years a Score,
Dreams of a Gown of forty-four;

42

Imaginary Charms can find,
In Eyes with Reading almost blind;
Cadenus now no more appears
Declin'd in Health, advanc'd in Years.
She fancies Musick in his Tongue,   530
Nor further looks, but thinks him young.
What Mariner is not afraid,
To venture in a Ship decay'd?
What Planter will attempt to yoke
A Sapling with a falling Oak?
As Years increase, she brighter shines,
Cadenus with each Day declines,
And he must fall a Prey to Time,
While she continues in her Prime.

    Cadenus, common Forms apart,   540
In every Scene had kept his Heart;
Had sigh'd and languish'd, vow'd, and writ,
For Pastime, or to shew his Wit;
But Time, and Books, and State Affairs
Had spoil'd his fashionable Airs;
He now cou'd praise, esteem, approve,
But understood not what was Love.
His Conduct might have made him styl'd
A Father, and the Nymph his Child.
That innocent Delight he took   550
To see the Virgin mind her Book,
Was but the Master's secret Joy
In School to hear the finest Boy.
Her Knowledge with her Fancy grew;
She hourly press'd for something new;
Ideas came into her Mind
So fast, his Lessons lagg'd behind:
She reason'd, without plodding long,

Nor ever gave her Judgment wrong.
But now a sudden Change was wrought.   560
She minds no longer what he taught.
Cadenus was amaz'd to find
Such Marks of a distracted Mind;
For tho' she seem'd to listen more
To all he spoke, than e'er before;
He found her Thoughts would absent range,
Yet guess'd not whence could spring the Change.
And first he modestly conjectures
His Pupil might be tir'd with Lectures;
Which help'd to mortify his Pride,   570
Yet gave him not the Heart to chide;
But in a mild dejected Strain,
At last he ventur'd to complain:
Said, she shou'd be no longer teiz'd;
Might have her Freedom when she pleas'd:
Was now convinc'd he acted wrong,
To hide her from the World so long;
And in dull Studies to engage
One of her tender Sex and Age.
That ev'ry Nymph with Envy own'd,   580
How she might shine in the *Grand-Monde*,
And ev'ry Shepherd was undone
To see her cloister'd like a Nun.
This was a visionary Scheme,
He wak'd, and found it but a Dream;
A Project far above his Skill,
For Nature must be Nature still.
If he was bolder than became
A Scholar to a Courtly Dame,
She might excuse a Man of Letters;   590
Thus Tutors often treat their Betters.
And since his Talk offensive grew,
He came to take his last Adieu.

Vanessa, fill'd with just Disdain,
Wou'd still her Dignity maintain,
Instructed from her early Years
To scorn the Art of Female Tears.

Had he employ'd his Time so long,
To teach her what was Right or Wrong,
Yet cou'd such Notions entertain,   600
That all his Lectures were in vain?
She own'd the wand'ring of her Thoughts,
But he must answer for her Faults.
She well remember'd to her Cost,
That all his Lessons were not lost.
Two Maxims she could still produce,
And sad Experience taught their Use:
That Virtue, pleas'd by being shown,
Knows nothing which it dare not own;
Can make us without Fear disclose   610
Our inmost Secrets to our Foes:
That common Forms were not design'd
Directors to a noble Mind.
Now, said the Nymph, I'll let you see
My Actions with your Rules agree,
That I can vulgar Forms despise,
And have no Secrets to disguise.
I knew by what you said and writ,
How dang'rous Things were Men of Wit,
You caution'd me against their Charms,   620
But never gave me equal Arms:
Your Lessons found the weakest Part,
Aim'd at the Head, but reach'd the Heart.

Cadenus felt within him rise
Shame, Disappointment, Guilt, Surprize.
He knew not how to reconcile
Such Language, with her usual Style:

And yet her Words were so exprest,
He cou'd not hope she spoke in Jest.
His Thoughts had wholly been confin'd   630
To form and cultivate her Mind.
He hardly knew, 'till he was told,
Whether the Nymph were Young or Old;
Had met her in a publick Place,
Without distinguishing her Face.
Much less could his declining Age
Vanessa's earliest Thoughts engage.
And if her Youth Indifference met,
His Person must Contempt beget.
Or grant her Passion be sincere,   640
How shall his Innocence be clear?
Appearances were all so strong,
The World must think him in the Wrong;
Wou'd say, He made a treach'rous Use
Of Wit, to flatter and seduce:
The Town wou'd swear he had betray'd,
By Magick Spells, the harmless Maid;
And ev'ry Beau wou'd have his Jokes,
That Scholars were like other Folks:
That when Platonick Flights were over,   650
The Tutor turn'd a mortal Lover.
So tender of the Young and Fair?
It shew'd a true Paternal Care—
Five thousand Guineas in her Purse?
The Doctor might have fancy'd worse.—

Hardly at length he Silence broke,
And faulter'd ev'ry Word he spoke;
Interpreting her Complaisance,
Just as a Man *sans Consequence*.
She railly'd well, he always knew,   660
Her Manner now was something new;

46

And what she spoke was in an Air,
As serious as a Tragick Play'r.
But those who aim at Ridicule
Shou'd fix upon some certain Rule,
Which fairly hints they are in jest,
Else he must enter his Protest:
For, let a Man be ne'er so wise,
He may be caught with sober Lies;
A Science which he never taught,   670
And, to be free, was dearly bought:
For, take it in its proper Light,
'Tis just what Coxcombs call, *a Bite*.

   But not to dwell on Things minute,
Vanessa finish'd the Dispute,
Brought weighty Arguments to prove
That Reason was her Guide in Love.
She thought he had himself describ'd,
His Doctrines when she first imbib'd;
What he had planted, now was grown;   680
His Virtues she might call her own;
As he approves, as he dislikes,
Love or Contempt, her Fancy strikes.
Self-Love, in Nature rooted fast,
Attends us first, and leaves us last:
Why she likes him, admire not at her,
She loves herself, and that's the Matter.
How was her Tutor wont to praise
The Genius's of ancient Days!
(Those Authors he so oft had nam'd   690
For Learning, Wit, and Wisdom fam'd;)
Was struck with Love, Esteem, and Awe,
For Persons whom he never saw.
Suppose *Cadenus* flourish'd then,
He must adore such God-like Men.

If one short Volume cou'd comprise
All that was witty, learn'd, and wise,
How wou'd it be esteem'd, and read,
Altho' the Writer long were dead?
If such an Author were alive,   700
How all wou'd for his Friendship strive;
And come in Crowds to see his Face:
And this she takes to be her Case.
Cadenus answers every End,
The Book, the Author, and the Friend.
The utmost her Desires will reach,
Is but to learn what he can teach·
His Converse is a System, fit
Alone to fill up all her Wit;
While ev'ry Passion of her Mind   710
In him is center'd and confin'd.

Love can with Speech inspire a Mute,
And taught *Vanessa* to dispute.
This Topick, never touch'd before,
Display'd her Eloquence the more:
Her Knowledge, with such Pains acquir'd,
By this new Passion grew inspir'd.
Thro' this she made all Objects pass,
Which gave a Tincture o'er the Mass:
As Rivers, tho' they bend and twine,   720
Still to the Sea their Course incline;
Or, as Philosophers, who find
Some fav'rite System to their Mind,
In ev'ry Point to make it fit,
Will force all Nature to submit.

Cadenus, who cou'd ne'er suspect
His Lessons wou'd have such Effect,
Or be so artfully apply'd,
Insensibly came on her Side;

48

It was an unforeseen Event,   730
Things took a Turn he never meant.
Whoe'er excels in what we prize,
Appears a Hero to our Eyes;
Each Girl when pleas'd with what is taught,
Will have the Teacher in her Thought.
When Miss delights in her Spinnet,
A Fidler may a Fortune get;
A Blockhead with melodious Voice
In Boarding-Schools can have his Choice;
And oft' the Dancing-Master's Art   740
Climbs from the Toe to touch the Heart.
In Learning let a Nymph delight,
The Pedant gets a Mistress by't.
Cadenus, to his Grief and Shame,
Cou'd scarce oppose *Vanessa*'s Flame;
But tho' her Arguments were strong,
At least, cou'd hardly wish them wrong.
Howe'er it came, he cou'd not tell,
But, sure, she never talk'd so well.
His Pride began to interpose,   750
Preferr'd before a Crowd of Beaux,
So bright a Nymph to come unsought,
Such Wonder by his Merit wrought;
'Tis Merit must with her prevail,
He never knew her Judgment fail,
She noted all she ever read,
And had a most discerning Head.

'Tis an old Maxim in the Schools,
That Vanity's the Food of Fools;
Yet now and then your Men of Wit   760
Will condescend to take a Bit.

So when *Cadenus* could not hide,
He chose to justify his Pride;

Constr'ing the Passion she had shown,
Much to her Praise, more to his Own.
Nature in him had Merit plac'd,
In her, a most judicious Taste.
Love, hitherto a transient Guest,
Ne'er held Possession of his Breast;
So, long attending at the Gate,   770
Disdain'd to enter in so late.
Love, why do we one Passion call?
When 'tis a Compound of them all;
Where hot and cold, where sharp and sweet,
In all their Equipages meet;
Where Pleasures mix'd with Pains appear,
Sorrow with Joy, and Hope with Fear.
Wherein his Dignity and Age
Forbid *Cadenus* to engage.
But Friendship in its greatest Height,   780
A constant, rational Delight,
On Virtue's Basis fix'd to last,
When Love's Allurements long are past;
Which gently warms, but cannot burn;
He gladly offers in return:
His Want of Passion will redeem,
With Gratitude, Respect, Esteem:
With that Devotion we bestow,
When Goddesses appear below.

    While thus *Cadenus* entertains   790
Vanessa in exalted Strains,
The Nymph in sober Words intreats
A Truce with all sublime Conceits.
For why such Raptures, Flights, and Fancies,
To her, who durst not read Romances;
In lofty Style to make Replies,
Which he had taught her to despise.

But when her Tutor will affect
Devotion, Duty, and Respect,
He fairly abdicates his Throne,   800
The Government is now her own;
He has a Forfeiture incurr'd,
She vows to take him at his Word,
And hopes he will not think it strange
If both shou'd now their Stations change.
The Nymph will have her Turn, to be
The Tutor; and the Pupil, he:
Tho' she already can discern,
Her Scholar is not apt to learn;
Or wants Capacity to reach   810
The Science she designs to teach:
Wherein his Genius was below
The Skill of ev'ry common Beau;
Who, tho' he cannot spell, is wise
Enough to read a Lady's Eyes;
And will each accidental Glance
Interpret for a kind Advance.

But what Success *Vanessa* met,
Is to the World a Secret yet:
Whether the Nymph, to please her Swain,   820
Talks in a high Romantick Strain;
Or whether he at last descends
To like with less Seraphick Ends;
Or, to compound the Business, whether
They temper Love and Books together;
Must never to Mankind be told,
Nor shall the conscious Muse unfold.

Mean time the mournful *Queen of Love*
Led but a weary Life above.
She ventures now to leave the Skies,   830
Grown by *Vanessa*'s Conduct wise.

For tho' by one perverse Event
Pallas had cross'd her first Intent,
Tho' her Design was not obtain'd,
Yet she had much Experience gain'd;
And, by the Project vainly try'd,
Cou'd better now the *Cause* decide.

She gave due Notice that both Parties,
Coram Regina prox' die Martis,
Should at their Peril without fail   840
Come and appear, and save their Bail.
All met, and Silence thrice proclaim'd,
One Lawyer to each Side was nam'd.
The Judge discover'd in her Face
Resentments for her late Disgrace;
And, full of Anger, Shame and Grief,
Directed them to mind their Brief;
Nor spend their Time to shew their Reading;
She'd have a summary Proceeding.
She gather'd, under ev'ry Head,   850
The Sum of what each Lawyer said;
Gave her own Reasons last; and then
Decreed the Cause against the *Men*.

But, in a weighty Case like this,
To shew she did not judge amiss,
Which evil Tongues might else report,
She made a Speech in open Court;
Wherein she grievously complains,
'How she was cheated by the Swains:
On whose Petition (humbly shewing   860
That Women were not worth the wooing,
And that unless the Sex would mend,
The Race of Lovers soon must end:)
"She was at Lord knows what Expence,
"To form a Nymph of Wit and Sense;

"A Model for her Sex design'd,
"Who never cou'd one Lover find.
"She saw her Favour was misplac'd;
"The Fellows had a wretched Taste;
"She needs must tell them to their Face,   870
"They were a senseless, stupid Race:
"And were she to begin agen,
"She'd study to reform the *Men*;
"Or add some Grains of Folly more
"To *Women* than they had before,
"To put them on an equal Foot;
"And this, or nothing else, wou'd do't.
"This might their mutual Fancy strike,
"Since ev'ry Being loves its *Like*.

"But now, repenting what was done,   880
"She left all Business to her Son:
"She puts the World in his Possession,
"And let him use it at Discretion."

The Cry'r was order'd to dismiss
The Court, so made his last *O yes!*
The Goddess wou'd no longer wait;
But rising from her Chair of State,
Left all below at Six and Sev'n,
Harness'd her Doves, and flew to Heav'n.

In Sickness

'TIS true,—then why should I repine,
To see my Life so fast decline?
But, why obscurely here alone?
Where I am neither lov'd nor known.
My State of Health none care to learn;
My Life is here no Soul's Concern.
And, those with whom I now converse,
Without a Tear will tend my Herse.
Remov'd from kind *Arbuthnot's* Aid,
Who knows his Art but not his Trade;   10
Preferring his Regard for me
Before his Credit or his Fee.
Some formal Visits, Looks, and Words,
What meer Humanity affords,
I meet perhaps from three or four,
From whom I once expected more;
Which those who tend the Sick for pay
Can act as decently as they.
But, no obliging, tender Friend
To help at my approaching End,   20
My Life is now a Burthen grown
To others, e'er it be my own.

YE formal Weepers for the Sick,
In your last Offices be quick:
And spare my absent Friends the Grief
To hear, yet give me no Relief;
Expir'd To-day, entomb'd To-morrow,
When known, will save a double Sorrow.

Mary the Cook-Maid's Letter to Dr Sheridan

WELL; if ever I saw such another Man since my Mother bound my Head,

You a Gentleman! marry come up, I wonder where you were bred?

I am sure such Words does not become a Man of your Cloth,

I would not give such Language to a Dog, faith and troth.

Yes; you call'd my Master a Knave: Fie Mr. *Sheridan*, 'tis a Shame

For a Parson, who shou'd know better Things, to come out with such a Name.

Knave in your Teeth, Mr. *Sheridan*, 'tis both a Shame and a Sin,

And the Dean my Master is an honester Man than you and all your kin:

He has more Goodness in his little Finger, than you have in your whole Body,

My Master is a parsonable Man, and not a spindle-shank'd hoddy doddy.   10

And now whereby I find you would fain make an Excuse,

Because my Master one Day in anger call'd you Goose.

Which, and I am sure I have been his Servant four Years since *October*,

And he never call'd me worse than Sweet-heart drunk or sober:

Not that I know his Reverence was ever concern'd to my knowledge,

Tho' you and your Come-rogues keep him out so late in your Colledge.

You say you will eat Grass on his Grave: a Christian eat Grass!

Whereby you now confess your self to be a Goose or an Ass:

But that's as much as to say, that my Master should die before ye,

Well, well, that's as God pleases, and I don't believe that's a true Story,   20

And so say I told you so, and you may go tell my Master; what care I?

And I don't care who knows it, 'tis all one to *Mary*.
Every body knows, that I love to tell Truth and shame the Devil,
I am but a poor Servant, but I think Gentle folks should be civil.
Besides, you found fault with our Vittles one Day that you was here,
I remember it was upon a *Tuesday*, of all Days in the Year.
And *Saunders* the Man says, you are always jesting and mocking,
Mary said he, (one Day, as I was mending my Master's Stocking,)
My Master is so fond of that Minister that keeps the School;
I thought my Master a wise Man, but that Man makes him a Fool. 30
Saunders said I, I would rather than a Quart of Ale,
He would come into our Kitchin, and I would pin a Dishclout to his
    Tail.
And now I must go, and get *Saunders* to direct this Letter,
For I write but a sad Scrawl, but my Sister *Marget* she writes better.
Well, but I must run and make the Bed before my Master comes
    from Pray'rs,
And see now, it strikes ten, and I hear him coming up Stairs:
Whereof I cou'd say more to your Verses, if I could write written
    hand,
And so I remain in a civil way, your Servant to command
                                                            Mary.

Phillis,
Or, the Progress of Love.

Desponding Phillis was endu'd
With ev'ry Talent of a Prude,
She trembled when a Man drew near;
Salute her, and she turn'd her Ear:
If o'er against her you were plac't
She durst not look above your Wast;

She'd rather take you to her Bed
Than let you see her dress her Head;
In Church you heard her thró the Crowd
Repeat the Absolution loud;   10
In Church, secure behind her Fan
She durst behold that Monster, Man:
There practic'd how to place her Head,
And bit her Lips to make them red:
Or on the Matt devoutly kneeling
Would lift her Eyes up to the Ceeling,
And heave her Bosom unaware
For neighb'ring Beaux to see it bare.

   At length a lucky Lover came,
And found Admittance from the Dame.   20
Suppose all Partyes now agreed,
The Writings drawn,the Lawyer fee'd,
The Vicar and the Ring bespoke:
Guess how could such a Match be broke.
See then what Mortals place their Bliss in!
Next morn betimes the Bride was missing,
The Mother scream'd, the Father chid,
Where can this idle Wench be hid?
No news of Phil. The Bridegroom came,
And thought his Bride had sculk't for shame,   30
Because her Father us'd to say
The Girl had such a Bashfull way.

   Now, John the Butler must be sent
To learn the Way that Phillis went;
The Groom was wisht to saddle Crop,
For John must neither light nor stop;
But find her where so'er she fled,
And bring her back, alive or dead.
See here again the Dev'l to do;
For truly John was missing too: 40

57

The Horse and Pillion both were gone
Phillis, it seems, was fled with John.
Old Madam who went up to find
What Papers Phil had left behind,
A Letter on the Toylet sees
To my much honor'd Father; These:
('Tis always done, Romances tell us,
When Daughters run away with Fellows)
Fill'd with the choicest common-places,
By others us'd in the like Cases.   50
That, long ago a Fortune-teller
Exactly said what now befell her,
And in a Glass had made her see
A serving-Man of low Degree:
It was her Fate; must be forgiven;
For Marriages are made in Heaven:
His Pardon begg'd, but to be plain,
She'd do't if 'twere to do again.
Thank God, 'twas neither Shame nor Sin,
For John was come of honest Kin: 60
Love never thinks of Rich and Poor,
She'd beg with John from Door to Door:
Forgive her, if it be a Crime,
She'll never do't another Time,
She ne'r before in all her Life
Once disobey'd him, Maid and Wife.
One Argument she summ'd up all in,
The Thing was done and past recalling:
And therefore hop'd she would recover
His Favor, when his Passion's over.   70
She valued not what others thought her;
And was—His most obedient Daughter.

    Fair Maidens all attend the Muse
    Who now the wandring Pair pursues:

Away they rode in homely Sort
Their Journy long, their Money short;
The loving Couple well bemir'd,
The Horse and both the Riders tir'd:
Their Vittells bad, their Lodging worse,
Phil cry'd, and John began to curse;   80
Phil wish't, that she had strained a Limb
When first she ventur'd out with him.
John wish't, that he had broke a Leg
When first for her he quitted Peg.

But what Adventures more befell 'um
The Muse has now not time to tell 'um.
How Jonny wheadled, threatned, fawnd,
Till Phillis all her Trinkets pawn'd:
How oft she broke her marriage Vows
In kindness to maintain her Spouse;   90
Till Swains unwholsome spoyld the Trade,
For now the Surgeon must be paid;
To whom those Perquisites are gone
In Christian Justice due to John.

When Food and Rayment now grew scarce
Fate put a Period to the Farce;
And with exact Poetick Justice:
For John is Landlord, Phillis Hostess;
They keep at Stains the old blue Boar,
Are Cat and Dog, and Rogue and Whore.   100

The Progress of Beauty

When first Diana leaves her Bed
Vapors and Steams her Looks disgrace,
A frouzy dirty colour'd red
Sits on her cloudy wrinckled Face.

But by degrees when mounted high
Her artificiall Face appears
Down from her Window in the Sky,
Her Spots are gone, her Visage clears.

'Twixt earthly Femals and the Moon
All Parallells exactly run;   10
If Celia should appear too soon
Alas, the Nymph would be undone.

To see her from her Pillow rise
All reeking in a cloudy Steam,
Crackt Lips, foul Teeth, and gummy Eyes,
Poor Strephon, how would he blaspheme!

The Soot or Powder which was wont
To make her Hair look black as Jet,
Falls from her Tresses on her Front
A mingled Mass of Dirt and Sweat.   20

Three Colours, Black, and Red, and White,
So gracefull in their proper Place,
Remove them to a diff'rent Light
They form a frightfull hideous Face,

For instance; when the Lilly slipps
Into the Precincts of the Rose,
And takes Possession of the Lips,
Leaving the Purple to the Nose.

So Celia went entire to bed,
All her Complexions safe and sound,   30
But when she rose, the black and red
Though still in Sight, had chang'd their Ground.

The Black, which would not be confin'd
A more inferior Station seeks
Leaving the fiery red behind,
And mingles in her muddy Cheeks.

The Paint by Perspiration cracks,
And falls in Rivulets of Sweat,
On either side you see the Tracks,
While at her Chin the Conflu'ents met.   40

A Skillfull Houswife thus her Thumb
With Spittle while she spins, anoints,
And thus the brown Meanders come
In trickling Streams betwixt her Joynts.

But Celia can with ease reduce
By help of Pencil, Paint and Brush
Each Colour to it's Place and Use,
And teach her Cheeks again to blush.

She knows her Early self no more,
But fill'd with Admiration, stands,   50
As Other Painters oft adore
The Workmanship of their own Hands.

Thus after four important Hours
Celia's the Wonder of her Sex;
Say, which among the Heav'nly Pow'rs
Could cause such wonderfull Effects.

Venus, indulgent to her Kind
Gave Women all their Hearts could wish
When first she taught them where to find
White Lead, and Lusitanian Dish.   60

Love with White lead cements his Wings,
White lead was sent us to repair
Two brightest, brittlest earthly Things
A Lady's Face, and China ware.

She ventures now to lift the Sash,
The Window is her proper Sphear;
Ah Lovely Nymph be not too rash,
Nor let the Beaux approach too near.

Take Pattern by your Sister Star,
Delude at once and Bless our Sight,   70
When you are seen, be seen from far,
And chiefly chuse to shine by Night.

In the Pell-mell when passing by,
Keep up the Glasses of your Chair,
Then each transported Fop will cry,
G—d d—m me Jack, she's wondrous fair.

But, Art no longer can prevayl
When the Materialls all are gone,
The best Mechanick Hand must fayl
Where Nothing's left to work upon.   80

Matter, as wise Logicians say,
Cannot without a Form subsist,
And Form, say I, as well as They,
Must fayl if Matter brings no Grist.

And this is fair Diana's Case
For, all Astrologers maintain
Each Night a Bit drops off her Face
When Mortals say she's in her Wain.

While Partridge wisely shews the Cause
Efficient of the Moon's Decay,   90
That Cancer with his pois'nous Claws
Attacks her in the milky Way:

But Gadbury in Art profound
From her pale Cheeks pretends to show
That Swain Endymion is not sound,
Or else, that Mercury's her Foe.

But, let the Cause be what it will,
In half a Month she looks so thin
That Flamstead can with all his Skill
See but her Forehead and her Chin.   100

Yet as she wasts, she grows discreet,
Till Midnight never shows her Head;
So rotting Celia stroles the Street
When sober Folks are all a-bed.

For sure if this be Luna's Fate,
Poor Celia, but of mortall Race
In vain expects a longer Date
To the Materialls of Her Face.

63

When Mercury her Tresses mows
To think of Oyl and Soot, is vain,   110
No Painting can restore a Nose,
Nor will her Teeth return again.

Two Balls of Glass may serve for Eyes,
White Lead can plaister up a Cleft,
But these alas, are poor Supplyes
If neither Cheeks, nor Lips be left.

Ye Pow'rs who over Love preside,
Since mortal Beautyes drop so soon,
If you would have us well supply'd,
Send us new Nymphs with each new Moon.   120

A Riddle

In Youth exalted high in Air,
Or bathing in the Waters fair;
Nature to form me took Delight,
And clad my Body all in White:
My Person tall, and slender Waste,
On either Side with Fringes grac'd;
Till me that Tyrant Man espy'd,
And drag'd me from my Mother's Side:
No Wonder now I look so thin;
The Tyrant strip't me to the Skin: 10
My Skin he flay'd, my Hair he cropt;
At Head and Foot my Body lopt:
And then, with Heart more hard than Stone,
He pick't my Marrow from the Bone.

To vex me more, he took a Freak,
To slit my Tongue, and made me speak:
But, that which wonderful appears,
I speak to Eyes and not to Ears.
He oft employs me in Disguise,
And makes me tell a Thousand Lyes: 20
To me he chiefly gives in Trust
To please his Malice, or his Lust.
From me no Secret he can hide;
I see his Vanity and Pride:
And my Delight is to expose
His Follies to his greatest Foes.

ALL Languages I can command,
Yet not a Word I understand.
Without my Aid, the best Divine
In Learning would not know a Line: 30
The Lawyer must forget his Pleading,
The Scholar could not shew his Reading.
Nay; Man, my Master, is my Slave:
I give Command to kill or save.
Can grant ten Thousand Pounds a Year,
And make a Beggar's Brat a Peer.

BUT, while I thus my Life relate,
I only hasten on my Fate.
My Tongue is black, my Mouth is furr'd,
I hardly now can force a Word.   40
I dye unpity'd and forgot;
And on some Dunghill left to rot.

Stella's Birth-Day (1725)

As when a beauteous Nymph decays
We say, she's past her Dancing Days;
So, Poets lose their Feet by Time,
And can no longer dance in Rhyme.
Your Annual Bard had rather chose
To celebrate your Birth in Prose;
Yet, merry Folks who want by chance
A Pair to make a Country Dance,
Call the Old Housekeeper, and get her
To fill a Place, for want of better; 10
While *S——n* is off the hooks,
And Friend *D——y* at his Books,
That *Stella* may avoid Disgrace
Once more the D——n supplies their Place.

Beauty and Wit, too sad a Truth,
Have always been confin'd to Youth;
The God of Wit, and Beauty's Queen,
He Twenty one, and She Fifteen:
No Poet ever sweetly sung,
Unless he were like *Phœbus*, young; 20
Nor ever Nymph inspir'd to Rhyme,
Unless, like *Venus*, in her Prime.
At Fifty six, if this be true,
Am I a Poet fit for you?
Or at the Age of Forty three,
Are you a Subject fit for me?
Adieu bright Wit, and radiant Eyes;
You must be grave, and I be wise.

Our Fate in vain we would oppose,
But I'll still be your Friend in Prose: 30
Esteem and Friendship to express,
Will not require Poetick Dress;
And if the Muse deny her Aid
To have them *sung*, they may be *said*.

But, *Stella* say, what evil Tongue
Reports you are no longer young?
That *Time* sits with his Scythe to mow
Where erst sate *Cupid* with his Bow;
That half your Locks are turn'd to Grey;
I'll ne'er believe a Word they say.   40
'Tis true, but let it not be known,
My Eyes are somewhat dimmish grown;
For Nature, always in the Right,
To your Decays adapts my Sight,
And Wrinkles undistinguish'd pass,
For I'm asham'd to use a Glass;
And till I see them with these Eyes,
Whoever says you have them, lyes.

No Length of Time can make you quit
Honour and Virtue, Sense and Wit,   50
Thus you may still be young to me,
While I can better *hear* than *see*;
Oh, ne'er may Fortune shew her Spight,
To make me *deaf*, and mend my *Sight*.

A Riddle

DEPRIV'D of Root, and Branch, and Rind,
Yet Flow'rs I bear of ev'ry Kind;
And such is my prolific Pow'r,
They bloom in less than half an Hour:
Yet Standers-by may plainly see
They get no Nourishment from me.
My Head, with Giddiness, goes round;
And yet I firmly stand my Ground:
All over naked I am seen,
And painted like an *Indian* Queen.   10
No Couple-Beggar in the Land
E'er join'd such Numbers Hand in Hand;
I join them fairly with a *Ring*;
Nor can our Parson blame the Thing:
And tho' no Marriage Words are spoke,
They part not till the *Ring* is broke.
Yet hypocrite Fanaticks cry,
I'm but an Idol rais'd on high;
And once a Weaver in our Town,
A damn'd *Cromwellian*, knock'd me down.   20
I lay a Prisoner twenty Years;
And then the Jovial Cavaliers
To their old Posts restor'd all Three,
I mean the Church, the King, and Me.

A Copy of Verses upon Two Celebrated Modern Poets

BEHOLD those Monarch-Oaks that rise,
With lofty Branches to the Skies,
Have large proportion'd Roots that grow
With equal Longitude below:
Two Bards that now in fashion reign,
Most aptly this Device explain:
If This to Clouds and Stars will venture,
That creeps as far to reach the Centre;
Or more to show the Thing I mean,
Have you not o'er a Sawpit seen,   10
A skill'd Mechanick that has stood,
High on a Length of prostrate Wood,
Who hir'd a subterraneous Friend,
To take his Iron by the End;
But which excell'd was never found,
The Man above, or under Ground.

The Moral is so plain to hit,
That had I been the God of Wit,
Then in a Sawpit and wet Weather,
Shou'd *Young* and *Phillips* drudge together.   20

Bec's Birth-Day

THIS day, dear Bec, is thy nativity,
Had fate a lucky'r one, she'd give it ye:
She chose a thread of greatest length
And doubly twisted it for strength;
Nor will be able with her shears
To cut it off these forty years.
Then, who says care will kill a cat?
Rebecca shews they're out in that.
For she, tho' over-run with care,
Continues healthy, fat, and fair.   10

As, if the gout should seize the head,
Doctors pronounce the patient dead;
But, if they can, by all their arts,
Eject it to th'extreamest parts,
They give the sick man joy, and praise
The gout that will prolong his days:
Rebecca thus I gladly greet,
Who drives her cares to hands and feet:
For, tho' philosophers maintain
The limbs are guided by the brain,   20
Quite contrary Rebecca's led,
Her hands and feet conduct her head,
By arbitrary pow'r convey her
She ne'er considers why, or where:
Her hands may meddle, feet may wander,
Her head is but a mere by-stander:
And all her bustling but supplies
The part of wholesome exercise:

Thus, nature hath resolv'd to pay her
The cat's nine lives and eke the care. 30

Long may she live, and help her friends
Whene'er it suits her private ends;
Domestic business never mind
'Till coffee has her stomach lin'd;
But, when her breakfast gives her courage,
Then, think on Stella's chicken porridge;
I mean when Tyger has been serv'd,
Or else poor Stella may be starv'd.

May Bec have many an evening nap
With Tyger slabb'ring in her lap; 40
But always take a special care
She does not overset the chair;
Still be she curious, never hearken
To any speech but Tyger's barking.

And, when she's in another scene,
Stella long dead, but first the Dean,
May fortune and her coffee get her
Companions that will please her better;
Whole afternoons will sit beside her,
Nor for neglects or blunders chide her; 50
A goodly set as can be found
Of hearty gossips prating round;
Fresh from a wedding, or a christ'ning,
To teach her ears the art of list'ning,
And please her more to hear them tattle
Than the Dean storm, or Stella rattle.

Late be her death, one gentle nod,
When Hermes, waiting with his rod,
Shall to Elysian fields invite her,
Where there will be no cares to fright her. 60

Stella's Birth-Day (1727)

THIS Day, whate'er the Fates decree,
Shall still be kept with Joy by me:
This Day then, let us not be told,
That you are sick, and I grown old,
Nor think on our approaching Ills,
And talk of Spectacles and Pills;
To morrow will be Time enough
To hear such mortifying Stuff.
Yet, since from Reason may be brought
A better and more pleasing Thought,   10
Which can in spite of all Decays,
Support a few remaining Days:
From not the gravest of Divines,
Accept for once some serious Lines.

Although we now can form no more
Long Schemes of Life, as heretofore;
Yet you, while Time is running fast,
Can look with Joy on what is past.

Were future Happiness and Pain,
A mere Contrivance of the Brain,   20
As Atheists argue, to entice,
And fit their Proselytes for Vice;
(The only Comfort they propose,
To have Companions in their Woes.)

Grant this the Case, yet sure 'tis hard,
That Virtue, stil'd its own Reward,
And by all Sages understood
To be the chief of human Good,
Should acting, die, nor leave behind
Some lasting Pleasure in the Mind,   30
Which by Remembrance will assuage,
Grief, Sickness, Poverty, and Age;
And strongly shoot a radiant Dart,
To shine through Life's declining Part.

Say, *Stella*, feel you no Content,
Reflecting on a Life well spent?
Your skilful Hand employ'd to save
Despairing Wretches from the Grave;
And then supporting with your Store,
Those whom you dragg'd from Death before: 40
(So Providence on Mortals waits,
Preserving what it first creates)
Your gen'rous Boldness to defend
An innocent and absent Friend;
That Courage which can make you just,
To Merit humbled in the Dust:
The Detestation you express
For Vice in all its glitt'ring Dress:
That Patience under tort'ring Pain,
Where stubborn Stoicks would complain.   50

Must these like empty Shadows pass,
Or Forms reflected from a Glass?
Or mere Chimæra's in the Mind,
That fly and leave no Marks behind?
Does not the Body thrive and grow
By Food of twenty Years ago?

73

And, had it not been still supply'd,
It must a thousand Times have dy'd.
Then, who with Reason can maintain,
That no Effects of Food remain?
And, is not Virtue in Mankind
The Nutriment that feeds the Mind?
Upheld by each good Action past,
And still continued by the last:
Then, who with Reason can pretend,
That all Effects of Virtue end?

Believe me *Stella*, when you show
That true Contempt for Things below,
Nor prize your Life for other Ends
Than merely to oblige your Friends;
Your former Actions claim their Part,
And join to fortify your Heart.
For Virtue in her daily Race,
Like *Janus*, bears a double Face;
Looks back with Joy where she has gone,
And therefore goes with Courage on.
She at your sickly Couch will wait,
And guide you to a better State.

O then, whatever Heav'n intends,
Take Pity on your pitying Friends;
Nor let your Ills affect your Mind,
To fancy they can be unkind.
Me, surely me, you ought to spare,
Who gladly would your Suff'rings share;
Or give my Scrap of Life to you,
And think it far beneath your Due;
You, to whose Care so oft I owe,
That I'm alive to tell you so.

Shall I Repine?

If neither brass nor marble can withstand
The mortal force of Time's dystructive hand
If mountains sink to vales, if cityes dye
And lessening rivers mourn their fountains dry
When my old cassock says a Welch divine
Is out at elbows why should I repine?

A Libel on Dr Delany and a Certain Great Lord

DELUDED Mortals, whom the *Great*
Chuse for Companions *tete à tete*,
Who at their Dinners, *en famille*
Get Leave to sit whene'er you will;
Then, boasting tell us where you din'd,
And, how his *Lordship* was so kind;
How many pleasant Things he spoke,
And, how you *laugh'd* at every *Joke:*
Swear, he's a most facetious Man,
That you and he are *Cup* and *Cann*.   10
You Travel with a heavy Load,
And quite mistake *Preferment's* Road.

Suppose my *Lord* and you alone;
Hint the least Int'rest of your own;
His Visage drops, he knits his Brow,

He cannot talk of Bus'ness now:
Or, mention but a vacant *Post*,
He'll turn it off with; *Name your Toast*.
Nor could the nicest Artist Paint,
A Countenance with more Constraint.   20

For, as their Appetites to quench,
Lords keep a Pimp to bring a Wench;
So, Men of Wit are but a kind
Of Pandars to a vicious Mind,
Who proper Objects must provide
To gratify their Lust of Pride,
When weary'd with Intrigues of State,
They find an idle Hour to Prate.
Then, shou'd you dare to ask a *Place*,
You Forfeit all your *Patron*'s Grace,   30
And disappoint the sole Design,
For which he summon'd you to *Dine*.

Thus, *Congreve* spent, in writing Plays,
And one poor Office, half his Days;
While *Montague*, who claim'd the Station
To be *Mæcenas* of the Nation,
For *Poets* open Table kept,
But ne'er consider'd where they Slept.
Himself, as rich as fifty *Jews*,
Was easy, though they wanted Shoes;   40
And, crazy *Congreve* scarce cou'd spare
A Shilling to discharge his Chair,
Till Prudence taught him to appeal
From *Pæan*'s Fire to *Party* Zeal;
Not owing to his happy Vein
The Fortunes of his latter Scene,
Took proper *Principles* to thrive;
And so might ev'ry *Dunce* alive.

Thus, *Steel* who own'd what others writ,
And flourish'd by imputed Wit,   50
From Lodging in a hundred Jayls,
Was left to starve, and dye in *Wales*.

Thus *Gay*, the *Hare* with many Friends,
Twice sev'n long Years the *Court* attends,
Who, under Tales conveying Truth,
To Virtue form'd a *Princely* Youth,
Who pay'd his Courtship with the Croud,
As far as *Modest Pride* allow'd,
Rejects a servile *Usher*'s Place,
And leaves *St. James*'s in Disgrace.   60

Thus *Addison* by Lords Carest,
Was left in Foreign Lands distrest,
Forgot at Home, became for Hire,
A trav'lling Tutor to a *Squire*;
But, wisely left the *Muses* Hill,
To Bus'ness shap'd the *Poet*'s Quil,
Let all his barren Lawrel's fade
Took up himself the *Courtier*'s Trade,
And grown a *Minister of State*,
Saw Poets at his Levee wait.   70

Hail! happy *Pope*, whose gen'rous Mind,
Detesting all the Statesmen kind,
Contemning *Courts*, at *Courts* unseen,
Refus'd the Visits of a Queen;
A Soul with ev'ry Virtue fraught
By *Sages*, *Priests*, or *Poets* taught;
Whose filial Piety excels
Whatever *Grecian* Story tells:
A Genius for all Stations fit,
Whose *meanest Talent* is his *Wit*:   80
His Heart too Great, though Fortune little,
To lick a *Rascal Statesman*'s Spittle.

Appealing to the Nation's Taste,
Above the Reach of Want is plac't;
By *Homer* dead was taught to thrive,
Which *Homer* never cou'd alive.
And, sits aloft on *Pindus* Head,
Despising *Slaves* that *cringe* for Bread.

   True *Politicians* only Pay
For solid Work, but not for Play;   90
Nor ever chuse to Work with Tools
Forg'd up in *Colleges* and *Schools*.
Consider how much more is due
To all their *Journey-Men*, than you,
At Table you can *Horace* quote;
They at a Pinch can bribe a Vote:
You shew your Skill in *Grecian* Story,
But, they can manage *Whig* and *Tory*:
You, as a *Critick*, are so curious
To find a Verse in *Virgil* Spurious;   100
But, they can *smoak* the deep Designs,
When *Bolingbroke* with *Pult'ney* Dines.

   Besides; your Patron may upbraid ye,
That you have got a Place already,
An Office for your Talents fit,
To Flatter, Carve, and shew your Wit;
To snuff the Lights, and stir the Fire,
And get a *Dinner* for your Hire,
What Claim have you to *Place*, or *Pension*?
He overpays in Condescension.   110

   But, Rev'rend *Doctor*, you, we know,
Cou'd never Condescend so low;
The *Vice-Roy*, whom you now attend,
Wou'd, if he durst, be more your Friend;
Nor will in you those Gifts despise,
By which himself was taught to rise:

78

When he has Virtue to retire,
He'll Grieve he did not raise you higher,
And place you in a better Station,
Although it might have pleas'd the Nation.   120

   This may be true—submitting still
To W—'s more than R—l Will.
And what Condition can be worse?
He comes to *drain* a *Beggar's Purse:*
He comes to tye our Chains on faster,
And shew us, *E——* is our Master:
Caressing Knaves and Dunces wooing,
To make them work their own undoing.
What has he else to bait his Traps,
Or bring his *Vermin* in, but *Scraps?*   130
The Offals of a *Church* distress't,
A hungry *Vicarage* at best;
Or, some remote inferior *Post*,
With forty Pounds a Year at most.

   But, here again you interpose;
Your favourite *Lord* is none of those,
Who owe their Virtues to their Stations,
And Characters to Dedications:
For keep him in, or turn him out,
His *Learning* none will call in doubt;   140
His *Learning*, though a *Poet* said it,
Before a Play, wou'd lose no Credit:
Nor POPE wou'd dare deny him Wit,
Although to Praise it PHILIPS Writ.
I own, he hates an Action base,
His *Virtues* battling with his *Place*;
Nor wants a nice discerning Spirit,
Betwixt a true and spurious Merit;
Can sometimes drop a *Voter's* Claim,
And give up Party to his Fame.   150

I do the most that *Friendship* can;
I hate the *Vice-Roy*, love the Man.

But, You, who till your Fortune's made
Must be a Sweet'ner by your Trade,
Shou'd swear he never meant us ill;
We suffer sore against his Will;
That, if we could but see his Heart,
He wou'd have chose a milder part;
We rather should Lament his Case
Who must Obey, or lose his *Place*.   160

Since this Reflection slipt your Pen,
Insert it when you write agen:
And, to Illustrate it, produce
This *Simile* for his Excuse.

"So, to destroy a guilty Land,
"An *Angel* sent by *Heav'n*'s Command,
"While he obeys *Almighty* Will,
"Perhaps, may feel *Compassion* still,
"And wish the Task had been assign'd
"To *Spirits* of less gentle kind.   170

But I, in *Politicks* grown old,
Whose Thoughts are of a diff'rent Mold,
Who, from my Soul, sincerely hate
Both —— and *Ministers* of *State*,
Who look on *Courts* with stricter Eyes,
To see the Seeds of *Vice* arise,
Can lend you an Allusion fitter,
Though *flatt'ring Knaves* may call it *bitter*.
Which, if you durst but give it place,
Would shew you many a *Statesman*'s Face.   180
Fresh from the *Tripod* of Apollo,
I had it in the Words that follow.
(Take Notice, to avoid Offence
I here except *His Excellence*.)

80

So, to effect his *M——h*'s ends,
From *Hell* a *V——* DEV'L ascends,
His *Budget* with *Corruptions* cramm'd,
The Contributions of the *damn'd*;
Which with unsparing Hand, he strows
Through *Courts* and *Senates* as he goes; 190
And then at *Beelzebub*'s *Black-Hall*,
Complains his *Budget* was too small.

Your *Simile* may better shine
In Verse; but there is *Truth* in mine.
For, no imaginable things
Can differ more than GOD and ——
And, *Statesmen* by ten thousand odds
Are ANGELS, just as —— are GODS.

Death and Daphne

To *an agreeable young Lady, but extremely lean*

DEATH went upon a solemn Day,
At *Pluto*'s Hall, his Court to pay:
The Phantom, having humbly kiss't
His griesly Monarch's sooty Fist,
Presented him the weekly Bills
Of Doctors, Fevers, Plagues, and Pills.
Pluto observing, since the Peace,
The Burial Article decrease;
And, vext to see Affairs miscarry,
Declar'd in Council, *Death* must marry: 10
Vow'd, he no longer could support
Old Batchelors about his Court:
The Int'rest of his Realm had need
That *Death* should get a num'rous Breed;

81

Young *Deathlings*, who, by Practice made
Proficient in their Father's Trade,
With Colonies might stock around
His large Dominions under Ground.

A CONSULT of Coquets below
Was call'd, to rig him out a Beau: 20
From her own Head, *Megæra* takes
A Perriwig of twisted Snakes;
Which in the nicest Fashion curl'd,
Like *Toupets* of this upper World;
(With Flow'r of Sulphur powder'd well,
That graceful on his Shoulders fell)
An Adder of the sable Kind,
In Line direct, hung down behind.
The Owl, the Raven, and the Bat,
Club'd for a Feather to his Hat;   30
His Coat, an Us'rer's Velvet Pall,
Bequeathed to *Pluto*, Corps and all.
But, loth his Person to expose
Bare, like a Carcase pick't by Crows,
A Lawyer o'er his Hands and Face,
Stuck artfully a Parchment Case.
No new-flux't Rake shew'd fairer Skin;
Not *Phyllis* after lying-in.
With Snuff was fill'd his Ebon Box,
Of Shin-Bones rotted by the Pox.   40
Nine Spirits of blaspheming Fops,
With Aconite anoint his Chops:
And give him Words of dreadful Sounds,
G—d—n his Blood, and Bl—— and W——ds.

THUS furnish't out, he sent his Train
To take a House in *Warwick* Lane:
The *Faculty*, his humble Friends,
A complimental Message sends:

Their President, in Scarlet Gown,
Harangu'd, and welcom'd him to Town.   50

BUT, *Death* had Bus'ness to dispatch:
His Mind was running on his Match.
And, hearing much of *Daphne*'s Fame,
His *Majesty of Terrors* came,
Fine as a Col'nel of the Guards,
To visit where she sat at Cards:
She, as he came into the Room,
Thought him *Adonis* in his Bloom.
And now her Heart with Pleasure jumps,
She scarce remembers what is Trumps.   60
For, such a Shape of Skin and Bone
Was never seen, except her own:
Charm'd with his Eyes and Chin and Snout,
Her Pocket-Glass drew slily out;
And, grew enamour'd with her Phiz,
As just the Counterpart of his.
She darted many a private Glance,
And freely made the first Advance:
Was of her Beauty grown so vain,
She doubted not to win the *Swain*.
Nothing she thought could sooner gain him,   70
Than with her Wit to entertain him.
She ask't about her Friends below;
This meagre Fop, that batter'd Beau:
Whether some late departed Toasts
Had got Gallants among the Ghosts?
If *Chloe* were a Sharper still,
As great as ever, at Quadrille?
(The Ladies there must needs be Rooks,
For, Cards we know, are *Pluto*'s Books)   80
If *Florimel* had found her Love
For whom she hang'd herself above?

How oft a Week was kept a Ball
By *Proserpine*, at *Pluto*'s Hall?
She fancy'd, those *Elysian* Shades
The sweetest Place for Masquerades:
How pleasant on the Banks of Styx,
To troll it in a Coach and Six!

WHAT Pride a Female Heart enflames!
How endless are Ambition's Aims!
Cease haughty Nymph; the Fates decree   90
Death must not be a Spouse for thee:
For, when by chance the meagre Shade
Upon thy Hand his Finger laid;
Thy Hand as dry and cold as Lead,
His matrimonial Spirit fled;
He felt about his Heart a Damp,
That quite extinguish't *Cupid*'s Lamp:
Away the frighted Spectre scuds,
And leaves my Lady in the Suds.   100

The Place of the Damn'd

ALL Folks who pretend to *Religion* and *Grace*,
Allow there's a HELL, but dispute of the Place;
But if HELL by *Logical* Rules be defin'd,
The Place of the *Damn'd*,—I'll tell you my Mind.
  Wherever the Damn'd do Chiefly abound,
Most certainly there's the HELL to be found,
Damn'd *Poets*, Damn'd *Criticks*, Damn'd *Block-Heads*, Damn'd
    Knaves,
Damn'd *Senators* brib'd, Damn'd prostitute *Slaves;*
Damn'd *Lawyers* and *Judges*, Damn'd *Lords* and Damn'd *Squires*,
Damn'd *Spies* and *Informers*, Damn'd *Friends* and Damn'd
    Lyars;   10

84

Damn'd *Villains*, Corrupted in every *Station*,
Damn'd *Time-Serving Priests* all over the *Nation;*
And into the Bargain, I'll readily give you,
Damn'd Ignorant *Prelates*, and *Councellors Privy*.
Then let us no longer by *Parsons* be Flam'd,
For We know by these *Marks*, the place of the Damn'd;
And HELL to be sure is at *Paris* or *Rome*,
How happy for *Us*, that it is not at *Home*.

Verses on the Death of Dr Swift

As *Rochefoucault* his Maxims drew
From Nature, I believe 'em true:
They argue no corrupted Mind
In him; the Fault is in Mankind.

THIS Maxim more than all the rest
Is thought too base for human Breast;
"In all Distresses of our Friends
"We first consult our private Ends,
"While Nature kindly bent to ease us,
"Points out some Circumstance to please us.   10

IF this perhaps your Patience move
Let Reason and Experience prove.

WE all behold with envious Eyes,
Our *Equal* rais'd above our *Size*;
Who wou'd not at a crowded Show,
Stand high himself, keep others low?

I love my Friend as well as you,
But would not have him stop my View;
Then let him have the higher Post;
I ask but for an Inch at most.   20

    If in a Battle you should find,
One, whom you love of all Mankind,
Had some heroick Action done,
A Champion kill'd, or Trophy won;
Rather than thus be over-topt,
Would you not wish his Lawrels cropt?

    DEAR honest *Ned* is in the Gout,
Lies rackt with Pain, and you without:
How patiently you hear him groan!
How glad the Case is not your own!   30

    WHAT Poet would not grieve to see,
His Brethren write as well as he?
But rather than they should excel,
He'd wish his Rivals all in Hell.

    HER End when Emulation misses,
She turns to Envy, Stings and Hisses:
The strongest Friendship yields to Pride,
Unless the Odds be on our Side.

    VAIN human Kind! Fantastick Race!
Thy various Follies, who can trace?   40
Self-love, Ambition, Envy, Pride,
Their Empire in our Hearts divide:
Give others Riches, Power, and Station,
'Tis all on me an Usurpation.
I have no Title to aspire;
Yet, when you sink, I seem the higher.

In POPE, I cannot read a Line,
But with a Sigh, I wish it mine:
When he can in one Couplet fix
More Sense than I can do in Six: 50
It gives me such a jealous Fit,
I cry, Pox take him, and his Wit.

WHY must I be outdone by GAY,
In my own hum'rous biting Way?

ARBUTHNOT is no more my Friend,
Who dares to Irony pretend;
Which I was born to introduce,
Refin'd it first, and shew'd its Use.

ST. JOHN, as well as PULTNEY knows,
That I had some repute for Prose;   60
And till they drove me out of Date,
Could maul a Minister of State:
If they have mortify'd my Pride,
And made me throw my Pen aside;
If with such Talents Heav'n hath blest 'em
Have I not Reason to detest 'em?

To all my Foes, dear Fortune, send
Thy Gifts, but never to my Friend:
I tamely can endure the first,
But, this with Envy makes me burst.   70

THUS much may serve by way of Proem,
Proceed we therefore to our Poem.

THE Time is not remote, when I
Must by the Course of Nature dye:
When I foresee my special Friends,
Will try to find their private Ends:

87

Tho' it is hardly understood,
Which way my Death can do them good;
Yet, thus methinks, I hear 'em speak;
See, how the Dean begins to break: 80
Poor Gentleman, he droops apace,
You plainly find it in his Face:
That old Vertigo in his Head,
Will never leave him, till he's dead:
Besides, his Memory decays,
He recollects not what he says;
He cannot call his Friends to Mind;
Forgets the Place where last he din'd:
Plyes you with Stories o'er and o'er,
He told them fifty Times before.   90
How does he fancy we can sit,
To hear his out-of-fashion'd Wit?
But he takes up with younger Fokes,
Who for his Wine will bear his Jokes:
Faith, he must make his Stories shorter,
Or change his Comrades once a Quarter:
In half the Time, he talks them round;
There must another Sett be found.

For Poetry, he's past his Prime,
He takes an Hour to find a Rhime: 100
His Fire is out, his Wit decay'd,
His Fancy sunk, his Muse a Jade.
I'd have him throw away his Pen;
But there's no talking to some Men.

And, then their Tenderness appears,
By adding largely to my Years:
"He's older than he would be reckon'd,
"And well remembers *Charles* the Second.

"He hardly drinks a Pint of Wine;
"And that, I doubt, is no good Sign.   110
"His Stomach too begins to fail:
"Last Year we thought him strong and hale;
"But now, he's quite another Thing;
"I wish he may hold out till Spring.

Then hug themselves, and reason thus;
"It is not yet so bad with us."

In such a Case they talk in Tropes,
And, by their Fears express their Hopes:
Some great Misfortune to portend,
No Enemy can match a Friend;   120
With all the Kindness they profess,
The Merit of a lucky Guess,
(When daily Howd'y's come of Course,
And Servants answer; *Worse and Worse*)
Wou'd please 'em better than to tell,
That, God be prais'd, the Dean is well.
Then he who prophecy'd the best,
Approves his Foresight to the rest:
"You know, I always fear'd the worst,
"And often told you so at first:"   130
He'd rather chuse that I should dye,
Than his Prediction prove a Lye.
Not one foretels I shall recover;
But, all agree, to give me over.

Yet shou'd some Neighbour feel a Pain,
Just in the Parts, where I complain;
How many a Message would he send?
What hearty Prayers that I should mend?
Enquire what Regimen I kept;
What gave me Ease, and how I slept?   140

89

And more lament, when I was dead,
Than all the Sniv'llers round my Bed.

MY good Companions, never fear,
For though you may mistake a Year;
Though your Prognosticks run too fast,
They must be verify'd at last.

BEHOLD the fatal Day arrive!
"How is the Dean? He's just alive.
Now the departing Prayer is read:
"He hardly breathes. The Dean is dead.   150
Before the Passing-Bell begun,
The News thro' half the Town has run.
"O, may we all for Death prepare!
"What has he left? And who's his Heir?"
"I know no more than what the News is,
"'Tis all bequeath'd to publick Uses."
"To publick Use! A perfect Whim!
"What had the Publick done for him!
"Meer Envy, Avarice, and Pride!
"He gave it all:—But first he dy'd.   160
"And had the Dean, in all the Nation,
"No worthy Friend, no poor Relation?
"So ready to do Strangers good,
"Forgetting his own Flesh and Blood?"

Now Grub-Street Wits are all employ'd;
With Elegies, the Town is cloy'd:
Some Paragraph in ev'ry Paper,
To *curse* the *Dean*, or *bless* the *Drapier*.

THE Doctors tender of their Fame,
Wisely on me lay all the Blame: 170
"We must confess his Case was nice;
"But he would never take Advice:

"Had he been rul'd, for ought appears,
"He might have liv'd these Twenty Years:
"For when we open'd him we found,
"That all his vital Parts were sound.

FROM *Dublin* soon to *London* spread,
'Tis told at Court, the Dean is dead.

KIND Lady *Suffolk* in the Spleen,
Runs laughing up to tell the Queen.   180
The Queen, so Gracious, Mild, and Good,
Cries, "Is he gone? 'Tis time he shou'd.
"He's dead you say; why let him rot;
"I'm glad the Medals were forgot.
"I promis'd them, I own; but when?
"I only was the Princess then;
"But now as Consort of the King,
"You know 'tis quite a different Thing.

Now, *Chartres* at Sir *Robert*'s Levee,
Tells, with a Sneer, the Tidings heavy: 190
"Why, is he dead without his Shoes?
(Cries *Bob*) "I'm Sorry for the News;
Oh, were the Wretch but living still,
And in his Place my good Friend *Will*;
Or, had a Mitre on his Head
Provided *Bolingbroke* were dead.

Now *Curl* his Shop from Rubbish drains;
Three genuine Tomes of *Swift*'s Remains.
And then to make them pass the glibber,
Revis'd by *Tibbalds, Moore, and Cibber*.   200
He'll treat me as he does my Betters.
Publish my Will, my Life, my Letters.
Revive the Libels born to dye;
Which POPE must bear, as well as I.

Here shift the Scene, to represent
How those I love, my Death lament.
Poor POPE will grieve a Month; and GAY
A Week; and ARBUTHNOTT a Day.

ST. JOHN himself will scarce forbear,
To bite his Pen, and drop a Tear.   210
The rest will give a Shrug and cry,
I'm sorry; but we all must dye.
Indifference clad in Wisdom's Guise,
All Fortitude of Mind supplies:
For how can stony Bowels melt,
In those who never Pity felt;
When *We* are lash'd, *They* kiss the Rod;
Resigning to the Will of God.

THE Fools, my Juniors by a Year,
Are tortur'd with Suspence and Fear.   220
Who wisely thought my Age a Screen,
When Death approach'd, to stand between:
The Screen remov'd, their Hearts are trembling,
They mourn for me without dissembling.

MY female Friends, whose tender Hearts
Have better learn'd to act their Parts.
Receive the News in *doleful Dumps*,
"The Dean is dead, (*and what is Trumps?*)
"Then Lord have Mercy on his Soul.
"(Ladies I'll venture for the *Vole*.)   230
"Six Deans they say must bear the Pall.
"I wish I knew what *King* to call.)
"Madam, your Husband will attend
"The Funeral of so good a Friend."
"No Madam, 'tis a shocking Sight,
"And he's engag'd To-morrow Night!

"My Lady *Club* wou'd take it ill,
"If he shou'd fail her at *Quadrill*.
"He lov'd the Dean. (*I lead a Heart.*)
"But dearest Friends, they say, must part.   240
"His Time was come, he ran his Race;
"We hope he's in a better Place.

WHY do we grieve that Friends should dye?
No Loss more easy to supply.
One Year is past; a different Scene;
No further mention of the Dean;
Who now, alas, no more is mist,
Than if he never did exist.
Where's now this Fav'rite of *Apollo*?
Departed; *and his Works must follow:*   250
Must undergo the common Fate;
His Kind of Wit is out of Date.
Some Country Squire to *Lintot* goes,
Enquires for SWIFT in Verse and Prose:
Says *Lintot*, "I have heard the Name:
"He dy'd a Year ago." The same.
He searcheth all his Shop in vain;
"Sir you may find them in *Duck-lane*:
"I sent them with a Load of Books,
"Last *Monday* to the Pastry-cooks.   260
"To fancy they cou'd live a Year!
"I find you're but a Stranger here.
"The Dean was famous in his Time;
"And had a Kind of Knack at Rhyme:
"His way of Writing now is past;
"The Town hath got a better Taste:
"I keep no antiquated Stuff;
"But, spick and span I have enough.
"Pray, do but give me leave to shew 'em;
"Here's *Colley Cibber*'s Birth-day Poem.   270

"This Ode you never yet have seen,
"By *Stephen Duck*, upon the Queen.
"Then, here's a Letter finely penn'd
"Against the *Craftsman* and his Friend;
"It clearly shews that all Reflection
"On Ministers, is disaffection.
"Next, here's Sir *Robert*'s Vindication,
"And Mr. *Henly*'s last Oration:
"The Hawkers have not got 'em yet,
"Your Honour please to buy a Set?   280

    "HERE'S *Wolston*'s Tracts, the twelfth Edition;
"'Tis read by ev'ry Politician:
"The Country Members, when in Town,
"To all their Boroughs send them down:
"You never met a Thing so smart;
"The Courtiers have them all by Heart:
"Those Maids of Honour (who can read)
"Are taught to use them for their Creed.
"The Rev'rend Author's good Intention,
"Hath been rewarded with a Pension: 290
"He doth an Honour to his Gown,
"By bravely running *Priest-craft* down:
"He shews, as sure as GOD's in *Gloc'ster*,
"That *Jesus* was a Grand Impostor:
"That all his Miracles were Cheats,
"Perform'd as Juglers do their Feats:
"The Church had never such a Writer:
"A Shame, he hath not got a Mitre!

    SUPPOSE me dead; and then suppose
A Club assembled at the *Rose*;   300
Where from Discourse of this and that,
I grow the Subject of their Chat:
And, while they toss my Name about,
With Favour some, and some without;

94

One quite indiff'rent in the Cause,
My Character impartial draws:

 "THE Dean, if we believe Report,
"Was never ill receiv'd at Court:
"As for his Works in Verse and Prose,
"I own my self no Judge of those: 310
"Nor, can I tell what Criticks thought 'em;
"But, this I know, all People bought 'em;
"As with a moral View design'd
"To cure the Vices of Mankind:
"His Vein, ironically grave,
"Expos'd the Fool, and lash'd the Knave:
"To steal a Hint was never known,
"But what he writ was all his own.

 "HE never thought an Honour done him,
"Because a Duke was proud to own him: 320
"Would rather slip aside, and chuse
"To talk with Wits in dirty Shoes:
"Despis'd the Fools with Stars and Garters,
"So often seen caressing *Chartres*:
"He never courted Men in Station,
"*Nor Persons had in Admiration*;
"Of no Man's Greatness was afraid,
"Because he sought for no Man's Aid.
"Though trusted long in great Affairs,
"He gave himself no haughty Airs: 330
"Without regarding private Ends,
"Spent all his Credit for his Friends:
"And only chose the Wise and Good;
"No Flatt'rers; no Allies in Blood;
"But succour'd Virtue in Distress,
"And seldom fail'd of good Success;
"As Numbers in their Hearts must own,
"Who, but for him, had been unknown.

"With Princes kept a due Decorum,
"But never stood in Awe before 'em: 340
"He follow'd *David*'s Lesson just,
"*In Princes never put thy Trust.*
"And, would you make him truly sower;
"Provoke him with *a slave in Power:*
"The *Irish* Senate, if you nam'd,
"With what Impatience he declaim'd!
"Fair LIBERTY was all his Cry;
"For her he stood prepar'd to die;
"For her he boldly stood alone;
"For her he oft expos'd his own.   350
"Two Kingdoms, just as Faction led,
"Had set a Price upon his Head;
"But, not a Traytor cou'd be found,
"To sell him for Six Hundred Pound.

"Had he but spar'd his Tongue and Pen,
"He might have rose like other Men:
"But, Power was never in his Thought;
"And, Wealth he valu'd not a Groat:
"Ingratitude he often found,
"And pity'd those who meant the Wound: 360
"But, kept the Tenor of his Mind,
"To merit well of human Kind:
"Nor made a Sacrifice of those
"Who still were true, to please his Foes.
"He labour'd many a fruitless Hour
"To reconcile his Friends in Power;
"Saw Mischief by a Faction brewing,
"While they pursu'd each others Ruin.
"But, finding vain was all his Care,
"He left the Court in meer Despair.   370

"And, oh! how short are human Schemes!
"Here ended all our golden Dreams.

"What St. John's Skill in State Affairs,
"What Ormond's *Valour*, Oxford's Cares,
"To save their sinking Country lent,
"Was all destroy'd by one Event.
"Too soon that precious Life was ended,
"On which alone, our Weal depended.
"When up a dangerous Faction starts,
"With Wrath and Vengeance in their Hearts: 380
"*By solemn League and Cov'nant bound,*
"To ruin, slaughter, and confound;
"To turn Religion to a Fable,
"And make the Government a *Babel*:
"Pervert the Law, disgrace the Gown,
"Corrupt the Senate, rob the Crown;
"To sacrifice old *England*'s Glory,
"And make her infamous in Story.
"When such a Tempest shook the Land,
"How could unguarded Virtue stand?   390

   "With Horror, Grief, Despair the Dean
"Beheld the dire destructive Scene:
"His Friends in Exile, or the Tower,
"Himself within the Frown of Power;
"Pursu'd by base envenom'd Pens,
"Far to the Land of Slaves and Fens;
"A servile Race in Folly nurs'd,
"Who truckle most, when treated worst.

   "By Innocence and Resolution,   400
"He bore continual Persecution;
"While Numbers to Preferment rose;
"Whose Merits were, to be his Foes.
"When, *ev'n his own familiar Friends*
"Intent upon their private Ends;
"Like Renegadoes now he feels,
"*Against him lifting up their Heels.*

"THE Dean did by his Pen defeat
"An infamous destructive Cheat.
"Taught Fools their Int'rest how to know;
"And gave them Arms to ward the Blow.   410
"Envy hath own'd it was his doing,
"To save that helpless Land from Ruin,
"While they who at the Steerage stood,
"And reapt the Profit, sought his Blood.

"To save them from their evil Fate,
"In him was held a Crime of State.
"A wicked Monster on the Bench,
"Whose Fury Blood could never quench;
"As vile and profligate a Villain,
"As modern *Scroggs*, or old *Tressilian*;   420
"Who long all Justice had discarded,
"Nor fear'd he GOD, nor Man regarded;
"Vow'd on the Dean his Rage to vent,
"And make him of his Zeal repent;
"But Heav'n his Innocence defends,
"The grateful People stand his Friends:
"Not Strains of Law, nor Judges Frown,
"Nor Topicks brought to please the Crown,
"Nor Witness hir'd, nor Jury pick'd,
"Prevail to bring him in convict.   430

"IN Exile with a steady Heart,
"He spent his Life's declining Part;
"Where, Folly, Pride, and Faction sway,
"Remote from ST. JOHN, POPE, and GAY.

"HIS Friendship there to few confin'd,
"Were always of the midling Kind:
"No Fools of Rank, a mungril Breed,
"Who fain would pass for Lords indeed:

98

"Where Titles give no Right or Power,
"And Peerage is a wither'd Flower,   440
"He would have held it a Disgrace,
"If such a Wretch had known his Face.
"On Rural Squires, that Kingdom's Bane,
"He vented oft his Wrath in vain:
"Biennial Squires, to Market brought;
"Who sell their Souls and Votes for Naught;
"The Nation stript go joyful back,
"To rob the Church, their Tenants rack,
"Go Snacks with Thieves and Rapparees,
"And, keep the Peace, to pick up Fees: 450
"In every Jobb to have a Share,
"A Jayl or Barrack to repair;
"And turn the Tax for publick Roads
"Commodious to their own Abodes.

   "PERHAPS I may allow, the Dean
"Had too much Satyr in his Vein;
"And seem'd determin'd not to starve it,
"Because no Age could more deserve it.
"Yet, Malice never was his Aim;
"He lash'd the Vice but spar'd the Name.   460
"No Individual could resent,
"Where Thousands equally were meant.
"His Satyr points at no Defect,
"But what all Mortals may correct;
"For he abhorr'd that senseless Tribe,
"Who call it Humour when they jibe:
"He spar'd a Hump or crooked Nose,
"Whose Owners set not up for Beaux.
"True genuine Dulness mov'd his Pity,
"Unless it offer'd to be witty.   470
"Those, who their Ignorance confess'd,
"He ne'er offended with a Jest;

"But laugh'd to hear an Idiot quote,
"A Verse from *Horace*, learn'd by Rote.

  "He knew an hundred pleasant Stories,
"With all the Turns of *Whigs* and *Tories:*
"Was chearful to his dying Day,
"And Friends would let him have his Way.

  "He gave the little Wealth he had,
"To build a House for Fools and Mad: 480
"And shew'd by one satyric Touch,
"No Nation wanted it so much:
"That Kingdom he hath left his Debtor,
"I wish it soon may have a Better.

Epigram on a Prelate leaving Church

Lord *Pam* in the Church (cou'd you think it) kneel'd down,
When told the Lieutenant was just come to Town,
His *Station* despising, unaw'd by the *Place*,
He flies from his *God*, to attend on his *Grace*:
To the *Court* it was fitter to pay his *Devotion*,
Since *God* had no Hand in his Lordship's *Promotion*.

On Poetry: A Rapsody

ALL Human Race wou'd fain be *Wits*,
And Millions miss, for one that hits.
Young's universal Passion, *Pride*,
Was never known to spread so wide.
Say *Britain*, cou'd you ever boast,——
Three *Poets* in an Age at most?
Our chilling Climate hardly bears
A *Sprig* of Bays in Fifty Years:
While ev'ry Fool his Claim alledges,
As if it grew in common Hedges.   10
What Reason can there be assign'd
For this Perverseness in the Mind?
Brutes find out where their Talents lie:
A *Bear* will not attempt to fly:
A founder'd *Horse* will oft debate,
Before he tries a five-barr'd Gate:
A *Dog* by Instinct turns aside,
Who sees the Ditch too deep and wide.
But *Man* we find the only Creature,
Who, led by *Folly*, fights with *Nature*;   20
Who, when *she* loudly cries, *Forbear*,
With Obstinacy fixes there;
And, where his *Genius* least inclines,
Absurdly bends his whole Designs.

Not *Empire* to the Rising-Sun,
By Valour, Conduct, Fortune won;

Nor highest *Wisdom* in Debates
For framing Laws to govern States;
Nor Skill in Sciences profound,
So large to grasp the Circle round;   30
Such heavenly Influence require,
As how to strike the *Muses Lyre*.

   Not Beggar's Brat, on Bulk begot;
Nor Bastard of a Pedlar *Scot;*
Nor Boy brought up to cleaning Shoes,
The Spawn of *Bridewell*, or the Stews;
Nor Infants dropt, the spurious Pledges
Of *Gipsies* littering under Hedges,
Are so disqualified by Fate
To rise in *Church*, or *Law*, or *State*,   40
As he, whom *Phebus* in his Ire
Hath *blasted* with poetick Fire.

   What hope of Custom in the *Fair*,
While not a Soul demands your Ware?
Where you have nothing to produce
For private Life, or publick Use?
Court, *City*, *Country* want you not;
You cannot bribe, betray, or plot.
For Poets, Law makes no Provision:
The Wealthy have you in Derision.   50
Of State-Affairs you cannot smatter,
Are awkward when you try to flatter.
Your Portion, taking *Britain* round,
Was just one annual Hundred Pound.
Now not so much as in Remainder
Since *Cibber* brought in an Attainder;
For ever fixt by Right Divine,
(A Monarch's Right) on *Grubstreet* Line.
Poor starv'ling Bard, how small thy Gains!
How unproportion'd to thy Pains!   60

And here a *Simile* comes Pat in:
Tho' *Chickens* take a Month to fatten,
The Guests in less than half an Hour
Will more than half a Score devour.
So, after toiling twenty Days,
To earn a Stock of Pence and Praise,
Thy Labours, grown the Critick's Prey,
Are swallow'd o'er a Dish of Tea;
Gone, to be never heard of more,
Gone, where the *Chickens* went before.   70

How shall a new Attempter learn
Of diff'rent Spirits to discern,
And how distinguish, which is which,
The Poet's Vein, or scribling Itch?
Then hear an old experienc'd Sinner
Instructing thus a young Beginner.

Consult yourself, and if you find
A powerful Impulse urge your Mind,
Impartial judge within your Breast
What Subject you can manage best;   80
Whether your Genius most inclines
To Satire, Praise, or hum'rous Lines;
To Elegies in mournful Tone,
Or Prologue sent from Hand unknown.
Then rising with *Aurora*'s Light,
The Muse invok'd, sit down to write;
Blot out, correct, insert, refine,
Enlarge, diminish, interline;
Be mindful, when Invention fails,
To scratch your Head, and bite your Nails.   90

Your Poem finish'd, next your Care
Is needful, to transcribe it fair.

In modern Wit all printed Trash, is
Set off with num'rous *Breaks*——and *Dashes*—

To Statesmen wou'd you give a Wipe,
You print it in *Italick Type*.
When Letters are in vulgar Shapes,
'Tis ten to one the Wit escapes;
But when in *Capitals* exprest,
The dullest Reader smoaks the Jest: 100
Or else perhaps he may invent
A better than the Poet meant,
As learned Commentators view
In *Homer* more than *Homer* knew.

Your Poem in its modish Dress,
Correctly fitted for the Press,
Convey by Penny-Post to *Lintot*,
But let no Friend alive look into't.
If *Lintot* thinks 'twill quit the Cost,
You need not fear your Labour lost: 110
And, how agreeably surpriz'd
Are you to see it advertiz'd!
The Hawker shews you one in Print,
As fresh as Farthings from the Mint:
The Product of your Toil and Sweating;
A Bastard of your own begetting.

Be sure at *Will*'s the following Day,
Lie Snug, and hear what Criticks say.
And if you find the general Vogue
Pronounces you a stupid Rogue;   120
Damns all your Thoughts as low and little,
Sit still, and swallow down your Spittle.
Be silent as a Politician,
For talking may beget Suspicion:

Or praise the Judgment of the Town,
And help yourself to run it down.
Give up your fond paternal Pride,
Nor argue on the weaker Side;
For Poems read without a Name
We justly praise, or justly blame: 130
And Criticks have no partial Views,
Except they know whom they abuse.
And since you ne'er provok'd their Spight,
Depend upon't their Judgment's right:
But if you blab, you are undone;
Consider what a Risk you run.
You lose your Credit all at once;
The Town will mark you for a Dunce:
The vilest Doggrel *Grubstreet* sends,
Will pass for yours with Foes and Friends.   140
And you must bear the whole Disgrace,
'Till some fresh Blockhead takes your Place.

Your Secret kept, your Poem sunk,
And sent in Quires to line a Trunk;
If still you be dispos'd to rhime,
Go try your Hand a second Time.
Again you fail, yet Safe's the Word,
Take Courage, and attempt a Third.
But first with Care imploy your Thoughts,
Where Criticks mark'd your former Faults.   150
The trivial Turns, the borrow'd Wit,
The *Similes* that nothing fit;
The *Cant* which ev'ry Fool repeats,
Town-Jests, and Coffee-house Conceits;
Descriptions tedious, flat and dry,
And introduc'd the Lord knows why;
Or where we find your Fury set
Against the harmless Alphabet;

On A's and B's your Malice vent,
While Readers wonder whom you meant.   160
A publick, or a private *Robber*;
A *Statesman*, or a South-Sea *Jobber*.
A *Prelate* who no God believes;
A ——, or Den of Thieves.
A Pick-purse at the Bar, or Bench;
A Duchess, or a Suburb-Wench.
Or oft when Epithets you link,
In gaping Lines to fill a Chink;
Like stepping Stones to save a Stride,
In Streets where Kennels are too wide: 170
Or like a Heel-piece to support
A Cripple with one Foot too short:
Or like a Bridge that joins a Marish
To Moorlands of a diff'rent Parish.
So have I seen ill-coupled Hounds,
Drag diff'rent Ways in miry Grounds.
So Geographers in *Afric*-Maps
With Savage-Pictures fill their Gaps;
And o'er unhabitable Downs
Place Elephants for want of Towns.   180

But tho' you miss your third Essay,
You need not throw your Pen away.
Lay now aside all Thoughts of Fame,
To spring more profitable Game.
From Party-Merit seek Support;
The vilest Verse thrives best at Court.
A Pamphlet in Sir *Rob*'s Defence
Will never fail to bring in Pence;
Nor be concern'd about the Sale,
He pays his Workmen on the Nail.   190

A Prince the Moment he is crown'd,
Inherits ev'ry Virtue round,

As Emblems of the sov'reign Pow'r,
Like other Bawbles of the Tow'r.
Is gen'rous, valiant, just and wise,
And so continues 'till he dies.
His humble *Senate* this professes,
In all their *Speeches, Votes, Addresses.*
But once you fix him in a Tomb,
His Virtues fade, his Vices bloom;   200
And each Perfection wrong imputed
Is Folly, at his Death confuted.
The Loads of Poems in his Praise,
Ascending make one Funeral-Blaze.
As soon as you can hear his Knell,
This God on Earth turns *Devil* in Hell.
And lo, his Ministers of State,
Transform'd to Imps, his Levee wait.
Where, in this Scene of endless Woe,
They ply their former Arts below.   210
And as they sail in *Charon*'s Boat,
Contrive to bribe the Judge's Vote.
To *Cerberus* they give a Sop,
His triple-barking Mouth to Stop:
Or in the Iv'ry Gate of Dreams,
Project * * * and * * * * * * *:
Or hire their Party-Pamphleteers,
To set *Elysium* by the Ears.

Then *Poet*, if you mean to thrive,
Employ your Muse on Kings alive;   220
With Prudence gath'ring up a Cluster
Of all the Virtues you can muster:
Which form'd into a Garland sweet,
Lay humbly at your Monarch's Feet;
Who, as the Odours reach his Throne,
Will smile, and think 'em all his own:

For *Law* and *Gospel* both determine
All Virtues lodge in royal Ermine.
(I mean the Oracles of Both,
Who shall depose it upon Oath.)   230
Your Garland in the following Reign,
Change but their Names will do again.

But if you think this Trade too base,
(Which seldom is the Dunce's Case)
Put on the Critick's Brow, and sit
At *Wills* the puny Judge of Wit.
A Nod, a Shrug, a scornful Smile,
With Caution us'd, may serve a-while.
Proceed no further in your Part,
Before you learn the Terms of Art: 240
(For you may easy be too far gone,
In all our modern Criticks Jargon.)
Then talk with more authentick Face,
Of *Unities, in Time and Place*.
Get Scraps of *Horace* from your Friends,
And have them at your Fingers Ends.
Learn *Aristotle*'s Rules by Rote,
And at all Hazards boldly quote:
Judicious *Rymer* oft review:
Wise *Dennis*, and profound *Bossu*.   250
Read all the *Prefaces* of *Dryden*,
For these our Criticks much confide in,
(Tho' meerly writ at first for filling
To raise the Volume's Price, a Shilling.)

A forward Critick often dupes us
With sham Quotations *Peri Hupsous*:
And if we have not read *Longinus*,
Will magisterially out-shine us.
Then, lest with *Greek* he over-run ye,
Procure the Book for Love or Money,   260

Translated from *Boileau*'s Translation,
And quote *Quotation* on *Quotation*.

   At *Wills* you hear a Poem read,
Where *Battus* from the Table-head,
Reclining on his Elbow-chair,
Gives Judgment with decisive Air.
To whom the Tribe of circling Wits,
As to an Oracle submits.
He gives Directions to the Town,
To cry it up, or run it down.   270
(Like *Courtiers*, when they send a Note,
Instructing *Members* how to Vote.)
He sets the Stamp of Bad and Good,
Tho' not a Word be understood.
Your Lesson learnt, you'll be secure
To get the Name of *Conoisseur*.
And when your Merits once are known,
Procure Disciples of your own.

   Our Poets (you can never want 'em,
Spread thro' *Augusta Trinobantum*)   280
Computing by their Pecks of Coals,
Amount to just Nine thousand Souls.
These o'er their proper Districts govern,
Of Wit and Humour, Judges sov'reign.
In ev'ry Street a City-bard
Rules, like an Alderman his Ward.
His indisputed Rights extend
Thro' all the Lane, from End to End.
The Neighbours round admire his *Shrewdness*,
For songs of *Loyalty* and *Lewdness*.   290
Out-done by none in Rhyming well,
Altho' he never learnt to spell.

Two bordering Wits contend for Glory;
And one is *Whig*, and one is *Tory*.
And this, for Epicks claims the Bays,
And that, for Elegiack Lays.
Some famed for Numbers soft and smooth,
By Lovers spoke in *Punch*'s Booth.
And some as justly Fame extols
For lofty Lines in *Smithfield* Drols.   300
Bavius in *Wapping* gains Renown,
And *Mævius* reigns o'er *Kentish-Town*:
Tigellius plac'd in *Phœbus*' Car,
From *Ludgate* shines to *Temple-bar*.
Harmonius *Cibber* entertains
The Court with annual Birth-day Strains;
Whence *Gay* was banish'd in Disgrace,
Where *Pope* will never show his Face;
Where *Y*---- must torture his Invention,
To flatter *Knaves*, or lose his *Pension*.   310

But these are not a thousandth Part
Of Jobbers in the Poets Art,
Attending each his proper Station,
And all in due Subordination;
Thro' ev'ry Alley to be found,
In Garrets high, or under Ground:
And when they join their *Pericranies*,
Out skips a *Book of Miscellanies*.
Hobbes clearly proves that ev'ry Creature
Lives in a State of War by Nature.   320
The Greater for the Smallest watch,
But meddle seldom with their Match.
A Whale of moderate Size will draw
A Shole of Herrings down his Maw.
A Fox with Geese his Belly crams;
A Wolf destroys a thousand Lambs.

But search among the rhiming Race,
The Brave are worried by the Base.
If, on *Parnassus'* Top you sit,
You rarely bite, are always bit: 330
Each Poet of inferior Size
On you shall rail and criticize;
And strive to tear you Limb from Limb,
While others do as much for him.

The Vermin only teaze and pinch
Their Foes superior by an Inch.
So, Nat'ralists observe, a Flea
Hath smaller Fleas that on him prey,
And these have smaller Fleas to bite 'em,
And so proceed *ad infinitum:*   340
Thus ev'ry Poet in his Kind,
Is bit by him that comes behind;
Who, tho' too little to be seen,
Can teaze, and gall, and give the Spleen;
Call Dunces, Fools, and Sons of Whores,
Lay *Grubstreet* at each others Doors:
Extol the *Greek* and *Roman* Masters,
And curse our modern Poetasters.
Complain, as many an ancient Bard did,
How Genius is no more rewarded;   350
How wrong a Taste prevails among us;
How much our Ancestors out-sung us;
Can personate an awkward Scorn
For those who are not Poets born:
And all their Brother Dunces lash,
Who crowd the Press with hourly Trash.

O, *Grubstreet!* how do I bemoan thee,
Whose graceless Children scorn to own thee!
Their filial Piety forgot,
Deny their Country like a SCOT: 360

Tho' by their Idiom and Grimace
They soon betray their native Place:
Yet *thou* hast greater Cause to be
Asham'd of them, than they of thee.
Degenerate from their ancient Brood,
Since first the Court allow'd them Food.

Remains a Difficulty still,
To purchase Fame by writing ill:
From *Flecknoe* down to *Howard*'s Time,
How few have reach'd the *low Sublime?*   370
For when our high-born *Howard* dy'd,
Blackmore alone his Place supply'd:
And least a Chasm should intervene,
When Death had finish'd *Blackmore*'s Reign,
The *leaden Crown* devolv'd to thee,
Great Poet of the *Hollow-Tree.*
But, oh, how unsecure thy Throne!
A thousand Bards thy Right disown:
They plot to turn in factious Zeal,
Duncenia to a Common-weal;   380
And with rebellious Arms pretend
An equal Priv'lege to *descend.*

In Bulk there are not more Degrees,
From *Elephants* to *Mites* in Cheese,
Than what a curious Eye may trace
In Creatures of the rhiming Race.
From bad to worse, and worse they fall,
But, who can reach the Worst of all?
For, tho' in Nature Depth and Height
Are equally held infinite,   390
In Poetry the Height we know;
'Tis only infinite below.
For Instance: When you rashly think,
No Rhymer can like *Welsted* sink.

112

His Merits ballanc'd you shall find,
That *Feilding* leaves him far behind.
Concannen, more aspiring Bard,
Climbs downwards, deeper by a Yard:
Smart JEMMY MOOR with Vigor drops,
The Rest pursue as thick as Hops: 400
With Heads to Points the Gulph they enter,
Linkt perpendicular to the Centre:
And as their Heels elated rise,
Their Heads attempt the nether Skies.

O, what Indignity and Shame
To prostitute the Muse's Name,
By flatt'ring — whom Heaven design'd
The Plagues and Scourges of Mankind.
Bred up in Ignorance and Sloth,
And ev'ry Vice that nurses both.   410

Fair *Britain* in thy Monarch blest,
Whose Virtues bear the strictest Test;
Whom never *Faction* cou'd bespatter,
Nor *Minister*, nor *Poet* flatter.
What Justice in rewarding Merit?
What Magnanimity of Spirit?
What Lineaments divine we trace
Thro' all the Features of his Face;
Tho' Peace with Olive bind his Hands,
Confest the conqu'ring Hero stands.   420
Hydaspes, *Indus*, and the *Ganges*,
Dread from his Hand impending Changes.
From him the *Tartar*, and *Chinese*,
Short by the Knees intreat for Peace.
The *Consort* of his Throne and Bed,
A perfect Goddess born and bred.
Appointed sov'reign Judge to sit
On Learning, Eloquence and Wit.

Our eldest Hope, divine *Iülus*,
(Late, very late, O, may he rule us.)   430
What early Manhood has he shown,
Before his downy Beard was grown!
Then think, what Wonders will be done
By going on as he begun;
An Heir for *Britain* to secure
As long as Sun and Moon endure.

The Remnant of the royal Blood,
Comes pouring on me like a Flood.
Bright Goddesses, in Number five;
Duke *William*, sweetest Prince alive.   440

Now sing the *Minister* of *State*,
Who shines alone, without a Mate.
Observe with what majestick Port
This *Atlas* stands to prop the Court:
Intent the Publick Debts to pay,
Like prudent *Fabius* by *Delay*.
Thou great Vicegerent of the King,
Thy Praises ev'ry Muse shall sing.
In all Affairs thou sole Director,
Of Wit and Learning chief Protector;   450
Tho' small the Time thou hast to spare,
The Church is thy peculiar Care.
Of pious Prelates what a Stock
You chuse to rule the Sable-flock.
You raise the Honour of the Peerage,
Proud to attend you at the Steerage.
You dignify the noble Race,
Content yourself with humbler Place.
Now Learning, Valour, Virtue, Sense,
To Titles give the sole Pretence.   460
St. George beheld thee with Delight,
Vouchsafe to be an azure Knight,

When on thy Breast and Sides *Herculean*,
He fixt the *Star* and *String Cerulean*.

   Say, Poet, in what other Nation,
Shone ever such a Constellation.
Attend ye *Popes*, and *Youngs*, and *Gays*,
And tune your Harps, and strow your Bays.
Your Panegyricks here provide,
You cannot err on Flatt'ry's Side.   470
Above the Stars exalt your Stile,
You still are low ten thousand Mile.
On *Lewis* all his Bards bestow'd,
Of Incense many a thousand Load;
But *Europe* mortify'd his Pride,
And swore the fawning Rascals ly'd:
Yet what the World refus'd to *Lewis*,
Apply'd to ------- exactly true is:
Exactly true! Invidious Poet!
'Tis fifty thousand Times below it.   480

   Translate me now some Lines, if you can,
From *Virgil*, *Martial*, *Ovid*, *Lucan*;
They could all Pow'r in Heaven divide,
And do no Wrong to either Side:
They'll teach you how to split a Hair,
Give ------- and *Jove* an equal Share.
Yet, why should we be lac'd so straight;
I'll give my ★★★★★ Butter-weight.
And Reason good; for many a Year
----- never intermeddl'd here: 490
Nor, tho' his Priests be duly paid,
Did ever we *desire* his Aid:
We now can better do without him,
Since *Woolston* gave us Arms to rout him.
★★★★★ *Cætera desiderantur* ★★★★★

His Curate's Complaint

I MARCH'D three miles thro' scorching sand,
With zeal in heart, and notes in hand;
I rode four more to great St. *Mary*;
Using four legs when two were weary.
To three fair virgins I did tie men
In the close bands of pleasing hymen.
I dipp'd two babes in holy-water,
And purify'd their mothers after.
Within an hour, and eke a half,
I preached three congregations deaf,   10
Which, thundring out with lungs long-winded,
I chopp'd so fast, that few there minded.
My Emblem, the labourious sun,
Saw all these mighty labours done,
Before one race of his was run;
All this perform'd by *Robert Hewit*,
What mortal else cou'd e'er go through it!

The Legion Club

As I strole the City, oft I
Spy a Building large and lofty,
Not a Bow-shot from the College,
Half the Globe from Sense and Knowledge.
By the prudent Architect
Plac'd against the Church direct;
Making good my Grandames Jest,
Near the Church—you know the rest.

TELL us, what this Pile contains?
Many a Head that holds no Brains.   10
These Demoniacs let me dub
With the Name of *Legion Club*.
Such Assemblies, you might swear,
Meet when Butchers bait a Bear;
Such a Noise, and such haranguing,
When a Brother Thief is hanging.
Such a Rout and such a Rabble
Run to hear Jackpudding gabble;
Such a Croud their Ordure throws
On a far less Villain's Nose.   20

COULD I from the Building's Top
Hear the rattling Thunder drop,
While the Devil upon the Roof,
If the Devil be Thunder Proof,
Should with Poker fiery-red
Crack the Stones, and melt the Lead;

Drive them down on every Scull,
While the Den of Thieves is full,
Quite destroy that Harpies Nest,
How might then our Isle be blest?
For Divines allow, that God
Sometimes makes the Devil his Rod:
And the Gospel will inform us,
He can punish Sins enormous.

YET should *Swift* endow the Schools
For his Lunaticks and Fools,
With a Rood or two of Land,
I allow the Pile may stand.
You perhaps will ask me, why so?
But it is with this Proviso,
Since the House is like to last,
Let a royal Grant be pass'd,
That the Club have Right to dwell
Each within his proper Cell;
With a Passage left to creep in,
And a Hole above for peeping.

LET them, when they once get in
Sell the Nation for a Pin;
While they sit a picking Straws
Let them rave of making Laws;
While they never hold their Tongue,
Let them dabble in their Dung;
Let them form a grand Committee,
How to plague and starve the City;
Let them stare and storm and frown,
When they see a Clergy-Gown.
Let them, 'ere they crack a Louse,
Call for th'Orders of the House;
Let them with their gosling Quills,
Scribble senseless Heads of Bills;

We may, while they strain their Throats,
Wipe our A—s with their V—.

LET Sir *T*—, that rampant Ass,
Stuff his Guts with Flax and Grass;
But before the Priest he fleeces
Tear the Bible all to Pieces.
At the Parsons, *Tom*, Halloo Boy,
Worthy Offspring of a Shoeboy,
Footman, Traytor, vile Seducer,
Perjur'd Rebel, brib'd Accuser;   70
Lay thy paltry Priviledge aside,
Sprung from Papists and a Regicide;
Fall a Working like a Mole,
Raise the Dirt about your Hole.

COME, assist me, Muse obedient,
Let us try some new Expedient;
Shift the Scene for half an Hour,
Time and Place are in thy Power.
Thither, gentle Muse, conduct me,
I shall ask, and you instruct me.   80

SEE, the Muse unbars the Gate;
Hark, the Monkeys, how they prate!

ALL ye Gods, who rule the Soul
Styx, through Hell whose Waters roll!
Let me be allow'd to tell
What I heard in yonder Hell.

NEAR the Door an entrance gapes,
Crouded round with antic Shapes;
Poverty, and *Grief*, and *Care*,
Causeless *Joy*, and true *Despair*;   90

Discord periwigg'd with Snakes,
See the dreadful Strides she takes.

By this odious Crew beset,
I began to rage and fret
And resolv'd to break their Pates,
'Ere we enter'd at the Gates;
Had not *Clio* in the Nick,
Whisper'd me, let down your Stick;
What, said I, is this the Mad-House?
These, she answer'd, are but Shadows,   100
Phantoms, bodiless and vain,
Empty Visions of the Brain.

In the Porch *Briareus* stands,
Shews a Bribe in all his Hands:
Briareus the Secretary,
But we Mortals call him *Cary*.
When the Rogues their Country fleece,
They may hope for Pence a Piece.

CLIO, who had been so wise
To put on a Fool's Disguise,   110
To bespeak some Approbation,
And be thought a near Relation;
When she saw three hundred Brutes,
All involv'd in wild Disputes;
Roaring till their Lungs were spent,
P-l-ge of P-l-m-nt,
Now a new Misfortune feels,
Dreading to be laid by th' Heels.
Never durst a Muse before
Enter that Infernal Door;   120
Clio stifled with the Smell,
Into Spleen and Vapours fell;

By the *Stygian* Steams that flew,
From the dire infectious Crew.
Not the Stench of Lake *Avernus*,
Could have more offended her Nose;
Had she flown but o'er the Top,
She would feel her Pinions drop,
And by Exhalations dire,
Though a Goddess must expire.   130
In a Fright she crept away,
Bravely I resolved to stay.

WHEN I saw the Keeper frown,
Tipping him with Half a Crown;
Now, said I, we are alone,
Name your Heroes one, by one.

WHO is that Hell-featur'd Brawler,
Is it Satan? No 'tis *W—*.
In what Figure can a Bard dress
Jack, the Grandson of Sir *Hardress*?   140
Honest Keeper, drive him further,
In his Looks are Hell and Murther;
See the Scowling Visage drop,
Just as when he murther'd *T—*.

KEEPER, shew me where to fix
On the Puppy Pair of *Dicks*;
By their lanthorn Jaws and Leathern,
You might swear they both are Brethren:
Dick Fitz-Baker, *Dick* the Player,
Old Acquaintance, are you there?   150
Dear Companions hug and kiss,
Toast *old Glorious* in your Piss.
Tye them Keeper in a Tether,
Let them stare and stink together;

Both are apt to be unruly,
Lash them daily, lash them duly,
Though 'tis hopeless to reclaim them,
Scorpion Rods perhaps may tame them.

KEEPER, yon old Dotard smoke,
Sweetly snoring in his Cloak.   160
Who is he? 'Tis hum-drum *W*—,
Half encompass'd by his Kin:
There observe the Tribe of *B*—*m*,
For he never fails to bring 'em;
While he sleeps the whole Debate,
They submissive round him wait;
Yet would gladly see the Hunks
In his Grave, and search his Trunks.
See they gently twitch his Coat,
Just to yawn, and give his Vote;   170
Always firm in his Vocation,
For the Court against the Nation.

THOSE are *A*—*s*, *Jack* and *Bob*,
First in every wicked Jobb,
Son and Brother to a Queer,
Brainsick Brute, they call a Peer.
We must give them better Quarter,
For their Ancestor trod Mortar;
And at *Hoath* to boast his Fame,
On a Chimney cut his Name.   180

THERE sit *C*—*s*, *D*—, and *H*—,
How they swagger from their Garrison.
Such a Triplet could you tell
Where to find on this Side Hell?
H—, and *D*—, and *C*—,
Souse them in their own Ex-crements.

Every Mischief in their Hearts,
If they fail 'tis Want of Parts.

BLESS us, *Morgan!* Art thou there Man?
Bless mine Eyes! Art thou the Chairman?   190
Chairman to yon damn'd Committee!
Yet I look on thee with Pity.
Dreadful Sight! What learned *Morgan*
Metamorphos'd to a Gorgan!
For thy horrid Looks, I own,
Half convert me to a Stone.
Hast thou been so long at School,
Now to turn a factious Tool!
Alma Mater was thy Mother,
Every young Divine thy Brother.   200
Thou a disobedient Varlet,
Treat thy Mother like a Harlot!
Thou, ungrateful to thy Teachers,
Who are all grown reverend Preachers!
Morgan! Would it not suprise one?
Turn thy Nourishment to Poison!
When you walk among your Books,
They reproach you with their Looks;
Bind them fast, or from the Shelves
They'll come down to right themselves: 210
Homer, Plutarch, Virgil, Flaccus,
All in Arms prepare to back us;
Soon repent, or put to Slaughter
Every *Greek* and *Roman* Author.
While you in your Faction's Phrase
Send the Clergy all to graze;
And to make your Project pass,
Leave them not a Blade of Grass.

How I want thee, humorous *Hogart?*
Thou I hear, a pleasant Rogue art;   220

Were but you and I acquainted,
Every Monster should be painted;
You should try your graving Tools
On this odious Group of Fools;
Draw the Beasts as I describe 'em,
Form their Features, while I gibe them;
Draw them like, for I assure you,
You will need no *Car'catura*;
Draw them so that we may trace
All the Soul in every Face.   230
Keeper, I must now retire,
You have done what I desire:
But I feel my Spirits spent,
With the Noise, the Sight, the Scent.

PRAY be patient, you shall find
Half the best are still behind:
You have hardly seen a Score,
I can shew two hundred more.
Keeper, I have seen enough,
Taking then a Pinch of Snuff;   240
I concluded, looking round 'em,
May their God, the Devil confound 'em.

An Epigram on Scolding

GREAT Folks are of a finer Mold;
Lord! how politely they can scold;
While a coarse *English* Tongue will itch,
For Whore and Rogue; and Dog and Bitch.

124

Verses made for *Women who cry Apples*, &c.

APPLES

Come buy my fine Wares,
Plumbs, Apples and Pears,
A hundred a Penny,
In Conscience too many,
Come, will you have any;
My Children are seven,
I wish them in Heaven,
My Husband's a Sot,
With his Pipe and his Pot,
Not a Farthing will gain 'em,   10
And I must maintain 'em.

ASPARAGUS

Ripe 'Sparagrass,
Fit for Lad or Lass,
To make their Water pass:
   O, 'tis pretty Picking
   With a tender Chicken.

ONYONS

Come, follow me by the Smell,
Here's delicate Onyons to sell,
I promise to use you well.
They make the Blood warmer,
You'll feed like a Farmer:

For this is ev'ry Cook's Opinion,
No sav'ry Dish without an Onyon;
But lest your Kissing should be spoyl'd,
Your Onyons must be th'roughly boyl'd;
    Or else you may spare   10
    Your Mistress a Share,
The Secret will never be known;
    She cannot discover
    The Breath of her Lover,
But think it as sweet as her own.

OYSTERS

Charming Oysters I cry,
My Masters come buy,
So plump and so fresh,
So sweet is their Flesh,
No *Colchester* Oyster,
Is sweeter and moyster,
Your Stomach they settle,
And rouse up your Mettle,
They'll make you a Dad
Of a Lass or a Lad;   10
And, Madam your Wife
They'll please to the Life;
Be she barren, be she old,
Be she Slut, or be she Scold,
Eat my Oysters, and lye near her,
She'll be fruitful, never fear her.

HERRINGS

Be not sparing,
Leave off swearing
Buy my Herring
Fresh from *Malahide*,
Better ne'er was try'd.

Come eat 'em with pure fresh Butter and Mustard,
Their Bellies are soft, and as white as a Custard.
Come, Six-pence a Dozen to get me some Bread,
Or, like my own Herrings, I soon shall be dead.

ORANGES

COME, buy my fine Oranges, Sauce for your Veal,
And charming when squeez'd in a Pot of brown Ale.
Well roasted, with Sugar and Wine in a Cup,
They'll make a sweet Bishop when Gentlefolks sup.

A Portrait from the Life

COME sit by my side, while this picture I draw:
In chatt'ring a magpie, in pride a jackdaw;
A temper the Devil himself could not bridle,
Impertinent mixture of busy and idle.
As rude as a bear, no mule half so crabbed;
She swills like a sow, and she breeds like a rabbit:
A house-wife in bed, at table a slattern;
For all an example, for no one a pattern.
Now tell me, friend Thomas, Ford, Grattan, and merry Dan,
Has this any likeness to good Madam Sheridan?   10

COMMENTARY AND NOTES

19. VERSES WROTE IN A LADY'S IVORY TABLE-BOOK (1698?)

*l.*10.   *Far an el breth:* The lady notes in her memorandum-book a remedy 'for an ill breath'. She suffers from halitosis.

*l.*21.   *Spittle and a Clout:* the lady's thoughts, written on the smooth ivory leaves of the book, may be erased by any fop who spits on a rag and writes down his own thoughts instead.

20. FRANCES HARRIS'S PETITION (1700)

Note that the full title may be read as the first two lines of the poem. *Harris* is the rhyme for *miscarries*.

The poem was written while Swift was chaplain in the household of Lord Berkeley who, with Lord Galway, was one of the Lords Justices of Ireland.

*l.*1.   *Lady Betty:* Lady Betty Berkeley, afterwards Germain.

*l.*23.   *Mrs. Dukes:* wife to one of the footmen.

*l.*24.   *Whittle:* valet to Lord Berkeley.

*l.*25.   *Dame Wadgar:* the old deaf housekeeper.

*l.*27.   *Collway:* i.e. Galway.

*l.*28.   *Dromedary:* Lord Drogheda, appointed to succeed Galway.

*l.*30.   *Cary:* Clerk of the Kitchen.

*l.*32.   *Steward:* named Ferris and regarded by Swift as a rogue.

*l.*38.   *three Skips of a Louse:* a common saying of Mrs. Harris.

*l.*45.   *Bedlam:* lunatic.

*l.*45.   *call'd her all to naught:* abused her violently.

*l.*48.   *Cunning Man:* one supposed to have the power of discovering a thief.

*l.*49.   *Chaplain:* i.e. Swift.

*l.*68.   *come to:* come to the point of proposing marriage. She is writing as if Swift were indeed her sweetheart, and she has insulted him by implying that he is a 'conjuror', i.e. one in league with the devil.

23. A BALLAD ON THE GAME OF TRAFFICK (1702)

The people mentioned in this glimpse of domestic life in Lord Berkeley's household are members of the household at Berkeley Castle in Gloucestershire.

129

l.8.   *Jack How:* John Grubham Howe, an ex-Whig who became a violent Tory, was twice M.P. for Gloucestrshire.

l.17.   *Herries:* Frances Harris, of the preceding poem.

ll.25.–28.   '*With these* . . .': Swift left the ballad unfinished, and this final stanza was contributed by Lady Betty.

24.   A DESCRIPTION OF THE MORNING (1709)

A piece of urban realism in ironical contrast to the usual poetic descriptions of morning in the country.

l.5.   *door:* i.e. doorstep.

l.9–10.   *The Youth* . . . The young man is scavenging in the gutter (*Kennel*) for odds and ends.

l.13.   *Duns:* debt-collectors. It is implied that Lords are usually in debt.

l.14.   *Brickdust:* used for scouring pans, cleaning knives, etc.

ll.15–16.   *The Turnkey* . . .: Gaolers accepted bribes to let their prisoners out at night for the purpose of pilfering.

25.   A DESCRIPTION OF A CITY SHOWER (1710)

Swift was very proud of this second piece of town description which, appearing in *The Tatler* in October 1710, earned him the praise of discriminating critics.

l.3.   *depends:* is imminent.

l.5.   *Sink:* (probably) a sewer.

l.10.   *Aches:* then pronounced as two syllables—*aitches.*

l.11.   *Dulman:* an imaginary grumbler.

ll.15–16.   *That swill'd* . . .: a simile borrowed from *The Tempest*, Act II Scene 2—'yond same black cloud . . . looks like a foul bombard that would shed his liquor'.

l.20.   *flirts:* flicks.

l.32.   *Devoted:* doomed, as by the Gods.

l.33.   *daggled:* mud-splashed.

l.34.   *cheapen:* bargain for.

l.38.   *Umbrella:* made of oiled silk, this was considered proper only for the use of women'.

l.51.   *Laoco'n:* see *Aeneid* II 50–53.

l.53.   *Kennels:* see previous poem, note on line 10.

l.58.   *Smithfield, or St. Pulchre's:* the cattle-market or St. Sepulchre's Church near Holborn Conduit. Here waters from Smithfield and Snow Hill join and fall into Fleet Ditch.

27.   CADENUS AND VANESSA (1712 or 1713)

'Vanessa', pseudonym of Esther Vanhomrigh (pronounced Vanummery) was one of the daughters of a Dutch merchant whose widow settled about

1707 in London, where Swift became acquainted with her. She was then nineteen or twenty years old. Swift ('Cadenus' is an anagram of Decanus: Dean) was then forty. She fell in love with him and after a long correspondence she followed him to Ireland in 1714 in the hope that Swift would reciprocate her passion. Her efforts failed, and she died in 1723. Swift wrote his long verse account of the growth of their friendship partly as a relief to his feelings and sent a copy to Vanessa. It was not intended for publication and did not appear during her lifetime.

l.2. *Cyprian Queen:* Venus. The poem opens in the pastoral convention, as a dispute at the court of the Queen of Love.

l.74. *the Bill:* the unnamed counsel for the defence of man asks that the action of the nymphs shall be dismissed, the fault being laid at the door of woman.

l.107. *Fleta's, Bractons, Cokes:* authorities on the law.

l.109. *To turn to Ovid . . .:* Ovid and Virgil are regarded as authorities on love: Tibullus, another Latin love poet of the 1st century B.C., like later English poets, is not regarded as authoritative.

l.122. *Imparlance:* a petition for an extension of time in pleading a case.

l.122. *Essoign:* legal term for delay.

l.126. *Clio.* Muse of History.

l.136. *Lucina:* one of the forms of the goddess Juno, under which she presided over childbirth.

l.137. *a wondrous Maid:* i.e. Vanessa.

l.155. *Amaranthine:* never-fading.

l.180. *Vanessa:* the pseudonym is a compound of the first syllable of Esther's surname and 'Essy', a diminutive form of Esther.

l.186. *Pallas:* goddess of wisdom, the quality to be added to beauty in the person of Vanessa.

l.190. *a boy:* Venus obtains wisdom for her protégée by pretending she is a boy.

l.250. *the Martial Maid:* Pallas was goddess of war as well as wisdom.

l.322. *Italian:* probably means an opera singer; opera was a fashionable mania at this time.

l.363. *But none . . .:* the meaning seems to be that she appears so stupid in the eyes of her idiotic admirers that she will escape the fate of witches usually regarded as wise women.

l.372. *Montaigne:* Swift much admired the 16th century French essayist.

l.385. *the Ring:* a riding course in Hyde Park.

l.417. *Colberteen:* a French lace named after the minister, Colbert.

l.431. *ombre:* card-game then in fashion.

l.503. *Grown old . . .:* during the last few years of Queen Anne's reign, when he was in his early forties, Swift achieved the apex of his political influence and was the intimate of St. John and Harley.

ll.524–5. Vanessa, not in Years . . .: these two lines would indicate 1711 as the date for the beginning of Vanessa's love.

l.574. teiz'd: harassed, plagued.

l.673: a Bite: a swindle.

l.763. Constr'ing: construing, interpreting.

l.839. Coram . . .: 'in the Queen's presence on Tuesday next'.

54. IN SICKNESS (1714)

An expression of Swift's depressed state of physical and mental health after his return to Ireland in the summer of 1714, when the death of Queen Anne and the fall of the Tory government had put an end to his worldly hopes.

l.9. Arbuthnot: Dr. John Arbuthnot, born in the same year as Swift, became physician to the Queen. He was the close friend of Swift as well as his medical adviser.

55. MARY THE COOK-MAID'S LETTER TO DR. SHERIDAN (1718)

Like *Frances Harris's Petition*, this delightful monologue shows Swift's inherent sympathy with servants and common people, as well as his infallible ear for racy popular speech. His cook Mary was a big robust woman with a homely, pock-marked face.

l.10. hoddy doddy: a short, squat fellow, with a possible suggestion of 'cuckold'.

l.15. concern'd: a euphemism for 'drunk'.

l.16. Come-rogues: drinking companions—evidently Mary's corruption of 'comrades'.

l.27. Saunders: Swift's name for his valued manservant Alexander McGee.

56. PHILLIS, OR, THE PROGRESS OF LOVE (1719)

60. THE PROGRESS OF BEAUTY (1719)

l.60. White Lead: used in cosmetics and in repairing china.

l.89. Partridge: a publisher of almanacks and quack astrologer, whom Swift took peculiar delight in satirising.

l.93. Gadbury: a noted astrologer.

l.96. Mercury: used in the treatment of syphilis.

l.99. Flamstead: John Flamsteed (*sic*), who died in 1719, was the first Astronomer Royal.

ll.109–115. These lines refer to the physical decay caused by venereal disease.

64. A RIDDLE (1724)

The circulation of ingenious riddles in verse was one of Swift's social amusements. This kind of verse is of primitive origin: examples still survive in Anglo-Saxon, and the rhyme of 'Humpty-Dumpty', known to all children, is a riddle of ancient origin. The answer to Swift's riddle is of course 'A quill pen'.

66. STELLA'S BIRTH-DAY (1725)

Stella was Swift's name for Esther Johnson (1681–1728), whom he first met in the household of Sir William Temple, which he entered as secretary about 1689. Swift and Stella formed a lifelong romantic attachment. About their relations every kind of inconclusive speculation has been made. What is certain is that his tender affection for her never wavered. He formed the habit of writing some verses for her on each of her birthdays. By 1725, the date of this example, she was forty-four.

l.11. For the blank supply Sheridan. Thomas Sheridan (1687–1738), a Dublin schoolmaster, was the close companion of Swift.

l.11. off the hooks: out of humour, out of spirits.

l.12. For the blank supply Delany. The Rev. Patrick Delany (1685?–1768), senior fellow and tutor of Trinity College, Dublin, was an intimate friend of Sheridan and Swift.

l.14. For the blank supply Dean.

68. A RIDDLE (1725)

Swift's defence of the maypole was a touch of passion over and above its wit and good humour. The maypole was associated with pagan spring rites and was attacked by Puritans ('Fanaticks') as leading to licentiousness and ungodly sexual behaviour. Swift refers to the Interregnum, or Commonwealth period, the twenty years between the beginning of the Civil War and the Restoration, as a time when 'Cromwellian weavers' persecuted most of the popular pastimes, such as dancing, ballad-singing and the May games. The weavers came from the Low Countries and settled in East Anglia, where they became some of Cromwell's staunchest adherents.

l.11. Couple-Beggar: a disreputable priest who performed irregular marriages.

69. A COPY OF VERSES UPON TWO CELEBRATED MODERN POETS (1729?)

l.10. Sawpit: Before the introduction of mechanical methods, tree-trunks were cut into planks in sawpits. One man stood above on the trunk, the other below in the pit. Together they worked a two-handed saw in long vertical strokes.

l.11. Mechanick: workman.

l.20. Young: Edward Young (1683–1765) was the author of *The Love of Fame, the Universal Passion*, which Swift had been reading about 1726.

Phillips: Ambrose Philips (1675?–1749) author of *Pastorals* and complimentary verses which gained him the nickname of 'Namby-Pamby Philips' was a frequent butt of Swift, Pope and their fellow-wits.

70. BEC'S BIRTH-DAY (1726)

Rebecca Dingley, a poor relation of Sir William Temple, was born about 1666 and died in 1743. She was Stella's lifelong companion.

*l.*37. *Tyger:* Mrs. Dingley's favourite lap-dog.

*l.*56. *rattle:* chatter.

72. STELLA'S BIRTH-DAY (13 March 1727)

This is Swift's last birthday poem to Stella, who died in January 1728. Shortly after writing it Swift left Dublin for his final visit to England. During the summer of 1727 Stella's last illness developed. Swift returned to Ireland in the autumn, and little is known about the final months of this lifelong friendship.

75. SHALL I REPINE? (1727?)

In this deflatory epigram Swift is commenting mock-heroically on grandiose notions of the power of time as expressed by Horace and in such poems as Shakespeare's Sonnet 65 ('Since brasse nor stone nor earth nor boundless sea...')

75. A LIBEL ON DOCTOR DELANY AND A CERTAIN GREAT LORD (1729)

Swift's friend Delany found his living in the north of Ireland, and one or two other minor church offices, insufficient for his needs. He accordingly applied for preferment to the Lord Lieutenant of Ireland, Lord Carteret, the 'certain great lord' of the poem. This was the occasion for Swift's impassioned attack on the whole system of preferment by political favour and on statesmen in general. The poem was not intended for publication at the time, though Swift was later annoyed with Pope for not including it ('the best thing I writ, as I think') in their joint *Miscellanies* of 1732. Pope regarded line 74 as endangering his own situation: he had no desire to get into trouble with the court. Swift's *Libel* was, however, circulated anonymously, and achieved immediate notoriety. The government almost prosecuted the author, but were no doubt restrained by consideration of the popularity of this sixty-two-year-old rebel against governmental tyranny. The power of Swift's attack on political patrons derives partly from his own bitter experience: in the reign of Queen Anne he had eaten out his heart in the fruitless pursuit of preferment worthy of his great talents and of the services he had rendered the government.

*l.*9. *facetious:* witty, amusing.

*l.*10. *Cup and Cann:* on terms of familiarity.

Notice the menacingly good-humoured, almost casual air of the opening of the poem, rendering all the more forceful the transition to bitter sarcasm.

*l.*24. *Pandar:* here Swift means a kind of intellectual pimp.

*ll.*33–48. Swift's account of relations between the dramatist Congreve and the statesman, Charles Montagu, Earl of Halifax, is hardly just. Congreve did in fact secure a number of lucrative sinecures in the civil service, and Halifax was a generous patron of literature. But Swift had fallen out with him.

*l.*36.   *Mæcenas:* a generic name for a patron of the arts. The original Mæcenas lived in the time of the Emperor Augustus, about 70–8 B.C.

*l.*41.   *crazy:* ruined, bankrupt (perhaps also 'ailing').

*l.*44.   *From Paean's Fire . . .:* Swift implies, erroneously, that Congreve turned from poetry to political propaganda.

*ll.*49–52.   *Thus, Steel . . .:* Swift's account of Steele is also fanciful. Steele's financial difficulties were mainly due to his own extravagance. He ran into debt, despite substantial political patronage, and retired to Carmarthen, where his second wife had property.

*ll.*53–60.   *Thus Gay . . .:* John Gay was the author of *Fables*, in one of which he compares himself to 'The Hare with many friends'. He was tutor to William, Duke of Cumberland (the 'Princely Youth') son of George II and later known as 'Butcher Cumberland'. Later Gay turned down the offer of a place as Gentleman Usher to the two-year-old Princess Louisa as being beneath his dignity.

*ll.*61–70.   *Thus Addison . . .:* Swift's account of Addison's career is partly but not wholly true.

*ll.*71–88.   *Hail! happy Pope . . .:* Pope always made much of his independence of patrons, and it is true that he achieved financial independence through his translations from Homer, which Swift had done much to encourage him in. He may have detested statesmen but he made frequent use of their services.

*ll.*89–102.   *True Politicians . . .:* Swift now turns to his friend Delany, who is a classical scholar and hence not welcome as the tool of ambitious and philistine politicians, who need more practical talents in their assistants.

*l.*101.   *smoak:* suspect, nose out—the implication being that if Bolingbroke dines with Pulteney, something is brewing.

*ll.*103–110.   *Besides; your Patron . . .:* Why do you need further preferment? You are already familiar enough with your patron to be allowed to dine with him on familiar terms.

*l.*122.   *W— . . . R—l:* Walpole . . . Royal. Swift is now about to attack directly, and in the most pungent satire, Walpole's vicegerent, the Lord Lieutenant of Ireland. Accordingly, when the satire first appeared, these textual abbreviations were necessary as some protection against a prosecution for libel. This even applies to the mention of England in line 126.

*l.*144.   *Philips:* Ambrose Philips, an enemy of Pope, had written a panegyric on Carteret in 1726.

*l.*152.   *I hate the Vice-Roy . . . :* This is very characteristic of Swift. He admits Carteret's qualities as a man but hates him as official representative of the English government.

*ll.*153–170.   *But, you who till your Fortune's made . . .:* Swift is ironically reproving Delany for not having made the usual excuse put forward for men like Carteret, that he is an enlightened man obliged to act tyranically because he is obeying orders. He is, as it were, an angel sent to do the devil's work. This clear-sighted condemnation of political expediency deserves to be better known.

*ll.*171–198. *But I, in Politicks . . .:* In this forthright peroration Swift boldly denounces the tools of kings as devils, not angels: a Viceroy, he says, is no more an angel than a king is a god.

*l.*174. *Both ——:* kings.

*l.*185. *M——h:* Monarch. Even here Swift had to be careful.

*l.*186. *V——:* Viceroy.

*l.*198. The blank of course stands for 'kings', as in 196.

81. DEATH AND DAPHNE (1730)

The lady was Lady Acheson, separated from her husband.

*l.*21. *Megæra:* one of the three Furies, sometimes represented as having snakes about them.

*l.*24. *Toupets:* wigs with long twisted tails.

*l.*37. *new flux't:* just purged.

*l.*42. *Aconite:* a poison.

*l.*46. *Warwick Lane:* in which was the College of Physicians in London.

*l.*65. *Phiz:* physiognomy, face.

*l.*79. *Rooks:* cheats.

*l.*87. *troll it:* roll round.

*l.*100. *in the Suds:* in perplexity, or in the sulks.

84. THE PLACE OF THE DAMN'D (1731)

*l.*15. *Flam'd:* deceived.

85. VERSES ON THE DEATH OF DR. SWIFT (1731)

Full title: 'Verses on the Death of Dr. Swift, D.S.P.D. occasioned by reading a maxim in Rochefoulcault. Dans l'adversité de nos meilleurs amis nous trouvons quelque chose, qui ne nous deplait pas. In the Adversity of our best Friends, we find something that doth not displease us.'

Swift had no intention of printing this poem when he wrote it. He told Pope it was not suitable for publication while he lived. However, unauthorized and cut versions appeared, and finally Swift allowed his Dublin publisher to issue it in a full and annotated version. Despite the ironical and playful tone of the poem, Swift, then, evidently took it seriously.

*l.*59. *St. John:* pronounced to rhyme with 'injun'. Henry St. John, Viscou **Boling**broke. Swift is over-modest. His prose is better than Bolingbroke's.

l.83. Vertigo: Swift suffered from labyrinthine vertigo, causing giddiness and deafness. The stress was on the second syllable in Swift's time.

l.108. Charles the Second: Swift was 18 when Charles II died.

l.117. Tropes: figures of speech—i.e... they speak indirectly.

l.156. publick Uses: Swift left the greater part of his money to found a mental hospital. St. Patrick's Hospital was opened in 1757.

l.165. Grub-Street Wits: hack writers, so called because they were supposed to live in the neighbourhood of this street, formerly in the neighbourhood of Moorfields.

l.168. Swift was the anonymous author of the *Drapier's Letters* (1724), by which was prevented the introduction of Wood's halfpence into Ireland, with ruinous effect upon the economy of the country.

l.179. Lady Suffolk: Mrs. Howard, later Countess of Suffolk, one of the Queen's ladies-in-waiting. She was genuinely friendly to Swift, who is here somewhat ironical at her expense.

l.184. Medals: according to Swift, the Queen promised him some medals, which however were never forthcoming.

l.189. Chartres: Francis Chartres (pronounced 'Charters') was an infamous rake and intimate with many ministers.

l.189. Sir Robert: ('Bob')—Walpole, when Prime Minister, was very civil to Swift but offended him by his treatment of Ireland, and Swift refused to see him again.

l.194. Will: William Pulteney had been a friend of Walpole but later opposed him in conjunction with Bolingbroke.

l.195. Mitre: the implication is that Swift would have been preferred to a bishopric but for his intimacy with Walpole's dangerous enemy Bolingbroke.

l.197. Curll: Edmund Curl, publisher, was a rogue but not so bad as he is represented in the writings of Swift and Pope. He did, however, publish a good many spurious works which were attributable to famous writers, including Swift and Pope.

l.200. Tibbalds, Moore, and Cibber: three authors attacked by Pope in the *Dunciad,* none (except perhaps Moore) as bad a writer as Swift and Pope made out.

l.202. Publish my Will, my Life, my Letters: Curll made a practice of issuing unauthorised editions of the letters, etc. of famous men.

l.230. Vole: a term in the card-game of quadrille.

ll.241–242. His Time was come . . .: Swift was fascinated, to the point of obsession, with the commonplaces of genteel conversation.

l.258. Duck-lane: lane where second-hand books were sold. Today we would say 'Charing Cross Road'.

l.260. Pastry-cooks: i.e. for lining pie-dishes, etc.

l.270. Here's Colley Cibber's . . .: In this and the following lines Swift imagines all the writers he most despises being in fashion after he has been forgotten. Cibber was Poet Laureate and therefore expected to write official odes for the King's birthday.

l.272. Stephen Duck: an agricultural labourer whose poems were taken up by fashionable circles. He was favoured by the Court, and this aroused ridicule and envy.

l.274. Craftsman: an anti-Whig weekly. *Friend:* Bolingbroke, co-founder of the *Craftsman.*

l.278. Henly: 'Orator' Henley, an eccentric clergyman.

l.281. Wolston: The Rev. Thomas Woolston (1670–1733), fellow of Sidney Sussex College, Cambridge, became a freethinker and wrote tracts, which became very popular, disputing, among other things, the authenticity of the miracles. He was deprived of his fellowship, tried for blasphemy and sent to prison, where he died.

l.300. the Rose: a tavern in Drury Lane, demolished later in the century.

l.307. 'The Dean, if we believe . . ': The following passage is Swift's account of himself as he wished to appear, put into the mouth of an unnamed admirer.

l.342. cf. Psalm 146 v. 3: 'Put not your trust in princes, nor in the son of man, in whom there is no help.'

l.351. Two Kingdoms . . .: Swift printed a note to these lines stating that substantial cash rewards were offered both in England and in Ireland to anyone who revealed the authorship of some of his most outspoken pamphlets, but no one could be found to betray him.

l.366. In 1714 Swift made strenuous but vain attempts to reconcile the two leading Tory ministers, Bolingbroke and Oxford, who were quarrelling.

l.374. Ormond: James Butler, Duke of Ormonde, appointed Commander-in-Chief when Marlborough was dismissed by the Tories in 1713.

l.377. that precious Life: the death of Queen Anne on 1 August 1714 found the Tory ministry in disarray. They never recovered power during Swift's lifetime.

l.381. solemn League and Cov'nant: the pact between English and Scottish Presbyterians in 1643, calling for the suppression of Roman Catholicism.

l.396. the Land of Slaves and Fens: Ireland, whither Swift retired on the failure of his political hopes.

ll.403–6. cf. Psalm 41 v. 9: 'Yea, mine own familiar friend, in whom I trusted . . . hath lifted up his heel against me.'

l.408. An infamous destructive Cheat: Wood, of the famous 'Wood's half-pence', by means of which Irish economy would have suffered had not Swift published the anonymous *Drapier's Letters.*

l.413. at the Steerage: at the helm (of the Ship of State).

l.417. A wicked Monster: Lord Chief Justice Whitshed sat in judgement in 1720 against the printer of one of Swift's pamphlets proposing the use throughout Ireland of home-produced goods. This angered commercial interests in England. The prosecution failed. Whitshed also judged in the subsequent prosecution of the printer of the Drapier's fourth letter: once again the jury refused to be intimidated, and the prosecution failed.

l.420. Scroggs: Chief Justice under Charles II. He was a mere tool of the Crown and was impeached by the Commons.

l.420. Tressilian: Chief Justice in 1381 after the suppression of the Peasant's Revolt. He ended up on the gallows.

l.427. Strains of Law: stretching the law.

l.445. Biennial Squires: Members of the Irish Parliament, which met only once in two years.

l.448. rack: extort high rents from.

l.449. Rapparees: highwaymen and plundering discharged soldiers.

l.449. Go Snacks: go shares.

l.451. Jobb: a racket.

ll.479–480. He gave the little Wealth . . .: see note on line 156.

100. EPIGRAM ON A PRELATE LEAVING CHURCH (1732?)

Full title: *Epigram. On seeing a worthy Prelate go out of Church in the Time of Divine Service, to wait on his Grace the D——— of D———.*

The prelate in question was the Rev. Josiah Hort, Bishop of Kilmore and Ardagh, later Archbishop of Tuam. Swift more than once satirized this divine on account of his blatant careerism. The Duke of Dorset was Lord Lieutenant of Ireland from 1730 to 1737 and from 1750 to 1755.

l.1. Lord Pam: Pam, the knave of clubs in, e.g. the card game of Loo, in which it is the highest trump—a sort of joker: 'the knave that picks up all.'

101. ON POETRY: A RAPSODY (1733)

From the time of its first anonymous appearance in London in 1733, this poem was always regarded as one of Swift's most forceful satires.

l.3. Young's universal Passion: Edward Young (1683–1765) published a collection of satires called *The Love of Fame, the Universal Passion.*

l.33. Bulk: a framework projecting from the front of a shop, a stall.

l.36. Bridewell . . . Stews: prison for vagrants and prostitutes . . . brothels.

l.41. Phebus: Apollo, the God of poets, whom Swift represents, half-seriously, half-ironically, as less favoured than the lowest of beings.

l.54. Hundred Pound: the annual stipend of the Poet Laureate was £100. Cibber was appointed to the position in 1730. Swift implies that Cibber brought the office into disrepute, entailing it upon Grub Street hack writers.

l.95. Wipe: a cutting rebuke. The implication is that italics will secure emphasis and attention.

l.100. smoaks: detects. Again the point is that capitals ensure close attention.

l.107.   *Lintot:* Bernard Lintot (b.1675) was the most famous publisher of his time.

l.117.   *Will's:* coffee-house frequented by Dryden and other men of letters, critics and wits.

l.139.   *The vilest Doggrel:* Swift, who always published anonymously, suffered much from the ascription to him of bad verse.

l.144.   *in Quires:* as unbound sheets.

l.162.   *South-Sea Jobber:* vendor of spurious commercial securities, as at the time of the South Sea Bubble, 1720.

l.164.   In place of Swift's blank, read 'Parliament'.

l.170.   *Kennels:* gutters.

l.173.   *Marish:* marsh.

l.187.   *Sir Rob:* Walpole.

l.197.   *Senate:* i.e. the Houses of Parliament.

l.216.   *Project . . . :* for Swift's blanks, read 'Excise' and 'South-Sea Schemes'.

l.235.   *Put on the Critick's brow . . . :* in the following passage, Swift supposes the would-be poet to have failed even as a hack versifier, and counsels him to set up as a critic, adopting suitable jargon. Dryden had written that 'The corruption of a poet is the generation of a critic'.

l.244.   *Unities, in Time and Place:* the so-called dramatic unities were the subject of much critical discussion during Swift's period.

l.245.   *Horace:* Horace's *De Artè Poetica*, a versified critical primer, was much in vogue.

l.247.   *Aristotle's Rules:* the dramatic unities were based on Aristotle's *Poetics*.

l.249.   *Rymer:* Thomas Rymer (1641–1713) had been a dramatic critic of some estimation in the time of Dryden.

l.250.   *Dennis . . . Bossu:* John Dennis (1657–1734) was a critic of some authority, at whose expense Swift and his friends were usually sarcastic, not entirely with justice. René le Bossu (1631–1680) was a French critic whose writings were of some influence in England at this time.

l.256.   *Peri Hupsous:* The treatise on *The Sublime* was attributed to the third century Greek critic Longinus. It was translated into French by Boileau about 1670 and became influential in later European critical theory.

l.264.   *Battus:* editors take this to refer to Dryden, who presided in his well-known armchair at Will's coffee-house. But Swift may mean any dictatorial critic, since Dryden had died in 1700.

l.280.   *Augusta Trinobantum:* the name for London after the Roman occupation.

l.300.   *Smithfield Drols:* street buffooneries or farces.

ll.301–302.   *Bavius . . . Mævius:* proverbial bad poets mentioned by Virgil.

l.304.   *Tigellius:* a musician favoured by Julius Caesar. Here simply another unnamed bad poet.

*l.*307. *Gay: Polly,* the sequel to Gay's highly successful *Beggar's Opera,* was considered offensive and the Court refused to have it licensed for performance.

*l.*309. *Y————:* Young was rewarded by Walpole in 1726 for his poem *The Instalment,* addressed to Walpole.

*l.*317. *Pericranies:* brains.

*l.*319. *Hobbes . . .:* The reference is to Hobbes's *Leviathan* (1651), which was highly influential on political thought in the succeeding period, and well known to Swift.

*l.*346. *Lay Grubstreet . . .:* accuse each other of bad writing.

*l.*369. *From Flecknoe . . .:* Richard Flecknoe and Edward Howard were bad 17th century poets.

*l.*372. *Blackmore:* Sir Richard Blackmore (d.1729), the author of a number of heavy epics, was a butt of Augustan wits.

*l.*376. *Great Poet:* Lord Grimston, author of the play *The Lawyer's Fortune, or Love in a Hollow Tree.*

*l.*380. *Duncenia:* the imaginary kingdom of Dullness, whose king Swift supposes a faction of citizens threaten to depose.

*l.*394. *Welsted:* Leonard Welsted (1688–1747), an underrated poet whose reputation has suffered from his inclusion in Pope's *Dunciad.*

*l.*396. *Feilding:* this name was inserted maliciously by Swift's enemies. Swift had in fact a high opinion of Feilding.

*l.*397. *Concannen:* Matthew Concanen (1701–1749) was also one of Pope's Dunces—a hack writer for Walpole's government.

*l.*399. *Jemmy Moor:* James Moore Smythe (1702–1734), a minor wit and satirist, also attacked in the *Dunciad.*

*l.*407. for the blank, supply 'Kings'.

*l.*411. *Fair Britain . . .:* The following account of George II is clearly ironical.

*l.*421. *Hydaspes, Indus . . .:* Swift is here suggesting the possibility of glorious conquests in the east.

*l.*429. *Iülus:* i.e. the Prince of Wales, Frederick Louis.

*l.*439. *Bright Goddesses:* the five daughters of George II and Queen Caroline.

*l.*440. *Duke William:* William Augustus, Duke of Cumberland.

*l.*441. *Now sing the Minister . . .:* a satirical portrait of Walpole.

*l.*442. *without a Mate:* presumably sarcastic. Walpole cared little for his notoriously unfaithful wife, and kept a mistress, Maria Skerrett.

*l.*446. *Fabius:* Fabius Cunctator, appointed dictator of Rome in 217 B.C., was proverbial for his policy of delay.

*l.*464. *the Star and String Cerulean:* the Order of the Garter, of which St. George was accounted patron.

*l.*473. *Lewis:* Louis XIV of France, the 'Roi Soleil'.

*ll.*478, 486.   For the blank supply 'George'.

l.488. For the blank supply 'Monarch'.

l.488. *Butter-weight:* formerly 18 or more ounces to the pound, hence 'good measure'.

l.490. For the blank supply either 'Jove' or 'God'.

l.495. *Cætera desiderantur:* 'the remaining lines are lacking'—an apology for the abrupt conclusion to the poem.

116. HIS CURATE'S COMPLAINT (1734?)

Full title: *Verses spoken extempore by Dean Swift on his Curate's Complaint of hard Duty.*

l.12. *chopp'd:* gabbled.

l.16. *Robert Hewit:* the actual name of the overworked curate of a parish in the neighbourhood of Swift's.

117. THE LEGION CLUB (1736)

Full title: *A Character, Panegyric, and Description of the Legion Club.*

Swift's last, and perhaps his most savage verse satire was a comprehensive attack on the Irish House of Commons, to which he gives the name of 'The Legion Club' after the reference in Mark 5, v. 9 to the Unclean Spirit which told Jesus his name was Legion, 'because many devils were entered into him'. Swift had long cherished grievances against the Irish parliament, which in effect acted as a colonial government in the interests of absentee landowners at the expense of the native population. The immediate occasion of *The Legion Club* was the passing by parliament of a measure absolving the landowners from paying tithes legally due to the clergy. So pointed and outspoken was this satire that no Dublin printer would run the risk of publishing it, and it first appeared in London. Many copies, however, circulated by hand in Ireland. Notice how the measure of the verse adds to its force and attack by the lack of unaccented syllables at the beginning of each line.

l.2. *a Building:* the new parliament building was begun in 1729 in the vicinity of Trinity College.

l.6. *the Church:* St. Andrew's.

l.7. *Grandames Jest:* 'Near the church and far from God'.

l.18. *Jackpudding:* buffoon, jester.

l.35. *Yet should Swift . . .:* Swift imagines the Irish members as some of the first inmates of the asylum he has endowed for lunatics.

l.63. *Sir T———:* Sir Thomas Prendergast, Bart. came of a Catholic family and became a Protestant and M.P. for Chichester and Clonmel.

l.64. *Flax and Grass:* products of agricultural Ireland, by which the landlords flourished.

l.65. *fleeces:* i.e. cheats the parson of his tithes.

*l.*97.   *Clio:* the Muse of History.

*l.*103.   *Briareus:* giant with a hundred hands.

*l.*106.   *Cary:* Walter Carey, formerly an English M.P., was principal secretary to the Lord Lieutenant, the Duke of Dorset.

*l.*116.   For the blanks supply 'Privilege of Parliament'.

*l.*122.   *Vapours:* similar to *Spleen*—morbid, often hypochondriac, depression.

*l.*125.   *Avernus:* a lake near Naples, supposed to be near the entrance to the underworld.

*l.*138.   *W—:* Lieutenant-Colonel John Waller, M.P. for Doneraile, was the grandson of Sir Hardess Waller, one of the judges at the trial of Charles I.

*l.*144.   *T———:* The Rev. Roger Throp had been persecuted by Waller, and these persecutions were believed to have hastened his death in January 1736.

*l.*146.   *Pair of Dicks:* (1) Richard Tighe, who was nicknamed Fitzbaker on account of his descent from a contractor who supplied bread to Cromwell's army, was an old political enemy of Swift.

(2) Richard Bettesworth, nicknamed 'the Player' on account of his pompous manner of speaking in the Irish parliament. He was hated by Swift on account of his support for anti-church legislation. So incensed was Bettesworth at Swift's continued verbal attacks on him in lampoons and ballads that he almost carried out his threat of cutting off Swift's ears with a penknife.

*l.*152.   *old Glorious:* Whig nickname used in praise of William III.

*l.*161.   *W———:* Three members of the Wynne family were at this time in the Irish parliament.

*l.*163.   *B——m:* Sir John and his brother Henry Bingham were also sitting in parliament.

*l.*167.   *Hunks:* surly person, bear, presumably Bingham, whose property the heirs are represented as coveting.

*l.*173.   *A——s:* John Allen was the son, and Robert Allen the brother of Viscount Allen, whose ancestor had been an architect in the service of Lord Howth.

*l.*181.   *C——s . . .:* other Irish M.P.'s of the families of Clements, Dilkes and Harrison.

*l.*189.   *Morgan:* Dr. Marcus Antonius Morgan was chairman of the committee of the Irish parliament which considered the landlords' petition against the payment of tithes to the clergy.

*l.*219.   *Hogart:* Swift appeals to the great English satirical painter and engraver, William Hogarth (1697–1764) for help in delineating the rogues and villains of the Irish parliament.

124.   AN EPIGRAM ON SCOLDING (date not known)

A typical piece of Swiftian realism commenting, as he frequently did, on the affectation of the polite world.

125. VERSES MADE FOR WOMEN WHO CRY APPLES, &C. (date not
      known)
Oysters
l.9. *They'll make you a Dad . . .*: It used to be widely believed that oysters
encourage virility.
Herrings
l.4. *Malahide:* a place about five miles from Dublin.
Oranges
l.4. *Bishop:* wine spiced with oranges or lemons and sugar.

127. A PORTRAIT FROM THE LIFE (date not known)
   This forthright description of the wife of his friend Dr. Thomas Sheridan is
evidently heartfelt. It was not published until after Swift's death. Sheridan's
wife, Elizabeth MacFadden, had money but was a slattern and a scold. In
1735 Sheridan wrote that he had been 'linked to the devil for twenty-four
years'.
l.9. *friend Thomas . . .*: Swift's friends, Thomas Sheridan, Charles Ford,
John Grattan and Daniel Jackson.

144

INDEX OF TITLES AND FIRST LINES
OF POEMS

145